Essay techniques in British government and politics

R. L. A. Tames MA (Cantab)
Chiswick Polytechnic

London · New York · St Louis · San Francisco · Düsseldorf
Johannesburg · Kuala Lumpur · Mexico · Montreal · New Delhi
Panama · Rio de Janeiro · Singapore · Sydney · Toronto

Published by
McGRAW-HILL Book Company (UK) Limited
MAIDENHEAD · BERKSHIRE · ENGLAND

07 094388 5

Copyright © 1972 McGraw-Hill Book Company (UK) Limited
All rights reserved. No part of this publication may be reproduced, stored in a retrieval system, or transmitted, in any form or by any means, electronic, mechanical, photocopying, recording, or otherwise, without the prior permission of McGraw-Hill Book Company (UK) Limited.

PRINTED AND BOUND IN GREAT BRITAIN

Contents

Preface	v
The nature of the British Constitution	1
What are the most important features of the British Constitution?	2
Explain and illustrate what is meant by the statement that Britain is governed by a unitary constitution.	3
Does the rule of law still exist?	5
To what extent does the hereditary principle survive in the British Constitution today and how can its survival be justified?	6
In what senses is Great Britain a democracy?	7
Make out a case for the retention of the Monarchy.	9
'Consultation is the essence of the modern Commonwealth.' Comment.	10
What factors would you expect to (a) strengthen and (b) weaken the Commonwealth?	11
The nature of British politics	13
How far do regional differences affect British politics?	14
What part do trade unions play in British politics?	15
Discuss the influence of religion on British politics.	17
'When it comes to politics the man in the street knows little and cares less.' Comment.	19
Elections and voting	21
What are the main disadvantages of the present electoral system?	22
What forms of proportional representation could be substituted for our present system of voting? Would such a reform be desirable?	23
How would you explain the fact that the Conservative Party attracts one-third of the working-class vote?	24
How do you account for the low turnout of voters at local elections? What could be done to raise the level of popular interest?	26
In what ways have the laws governing elections been altered in the last five years? What further changes could be made?	27
Parties and pressure groups	29
Do pressure groups assist or obstruct the working of democratic government?	30
How does public opinion make itself felt between general elections?	31
What is the difference between a political party and a pressure group?	32
'Mass parties are the creation of mass society.' Comment.	33
The Member of Parliament	35
What are the major attractions of an MP's job? Are there any features of backbench life which might discourage potential Parliamentary candidates?	36
Can a British MP be more accurately described as a representative than as a delegate?	37
How effectively can MPs exercise control over the actions of government departments?	39
Upon what sources of information can MPs draw?	41

Parliament 43
What, in fact, does the doctrine of the 'sovereignty of Parliament' imply? 44
'The procedure of the House of Commons is now a positive hindrance to good government.' How could the procedure be improved? 45
Discuss the role of the party Whips in Parliamentary government. 47
What is the role of the Opposition in the British political system? 48
Discuss the cases for and against televising debates from the House of Commons. 50
What are the propsects for the reform of the House of Lords? 51
What privileges does Parliament possess and why? 53
Why is the office of Speaker so important? 54

Central government 57
What were the main finding and recommendations of the Fulton Report? 58
What are the responsibilities of a British Prime Minister? 59
Consider the cases for and against a smaller Cabinet. 61
What is meant by 'collective responsibility'? Why is it important? 62
Discuss the development of administrative tribunals and the problems they have posed. 64

Local government 67
What were the main findings and recommendations of the *report on the management of local government?* 68
Consider the reasons for and against becoming a local councillor. 69
How can local government benefit from modern methods of management? 71
How could local government finance be reformed? 73
'Party politics should have no place in local government.' Discuss. 74

The law 77
Consider the cases for and against the present jury system. 78
In what ways have the courts acted to uphold the rule of law? 79
How does the British Constitution protect the personal liberty of the individual? 80
What limitations are there on freedom of speech in Britain? 81
'British justice may be impartially administered but only the rich can afford it.' Comment. 82
How are JPs recruited and trained? Could the system be improved? 83

Preface

The study of British government and politics has expanded very rapidly in the postwar period and is now included in the syllabus of most professional examining boards, as well as being one of the most popular subjects offered by the GCE examining boards. In addition to this expansion, the subject has undergone an internal revolution due to the impact of modern behavioural science and has moved away from a narrow, legalistic study of 'The British Constitution' towards a wider, but in many ways less clearly defined, survey and investigation of the workings of 'The British Political System'. This 'revolution' has by no means ended for the subject remains in a state of flux, which may help to account for the rather diverse nature of the essays in this book. A single examination paper may now invite the candidate to offer the traditional, terse discussion of the significance of constitutional conventions or to attempt an analysis of, say, voting behaviour or the impact of television on the modern party system. Papers also tend to vary in length and, while some require three essays, others ask for four or five. For this reason, answers of varying length have been included.

This book attempts to suggest by presenting a widely varied selection of full-length answers how essay questions may be tackled. Politics is an open-ended subject and there can be no final judgements. The essays in this book will, it is hoped, provide a starting point for thought and discussion. They do not present a shortcut to examination success. They make no concessions in the vocabulary or the concepts they use. References to authorities and specific persons or events will be lost on those who have failed to read widely or to digest what they have read.

How to use this book

(a) Use the essays as a basis for critical analysis and discussion. Examine them in depth and suggest ways in which they might be made more concise and coherent. The more dissatisfied you become with the essays in this book, the more you may be sure you are making progress.
(b) Prepare answers for questions taken from the Contents pages before reading the suggested answers. Contrast the two answers. Apart from checking whether any major points have been missed, compare the lines of argument which have been taken and the conclusions reached.
(c) Try setting your own examination paper. This exercise is most useful if carried out in co-operation with a fellow student, each of you attempting to test the other fairly. By putting yourself in the

examiner's place, you may come to appreciate the problems facing him and understand what he is looking for.

Your paper should:
(i) Cover the whole syllabus evenly.
(ii) Give opportunities for candidates to criticize and argue, showing more than routine knowledge and skill.

The aim should be to allow candidates to show what they do know rather than what they do not. Above all, remember that an examination should enable candidates to display powers of understanding rather than of memory.

Writing essays

(a) The first thing to decide is: What is the point of this question? What do I need to know to answer it?

(b) It is often advisable to make a brief, rough plan. This helps to cut out repetition, aids logical presentation, and gives time for second thought. When your plan is finished, look at it again and ask yourself whether you should attempt the question at all. At most, you will have lost only a few minutes. Once you start writing, you are committed. It becomes increasingly difficult to abandon an essay if you realize too late that you should never have started it.

(c) When writing, remember that conciseness and relevance are the two vital elements in a good essay.

(d) Do not 'name-drop', but feel free to cite particular writers by name if they are associated with a particular thesis, e.g., J. P. Mackintosh on regional government. Citing an eminent authority to back up a commonplace statement merely looks absurd. Moreover, there is little point in quoting the authors of standard texts. Equally pointless is the practice of memorizing lengthy quotations; an accurate paraphrase will be quite acceptable. Approximate statistics will also pass in most cases.

(e) Questions are often set in a deliberately 'loose' manner and a successful answer may depend on spotting ambiguous wording or a suspect definition, e.g., 'average' or 'typical', 'voter' and 'pressure group', all may need careful handling.

It may often be necessary to start an essay by indicating the background. Care should be taken that this does not involve more than a paragraph. To write more would make the answer unbalanced or make it look as though you only knew about a related topic and were, therefore, determined to write about that.

(f) Try to reach a conclusion which is in itself a stopping point. It may clinch the whole argument or set it in a wider context. Either way, it should not be a repetitious summary of what has gone before.

(g) Always re-read. It may be depressing, but it gives you the opportunity to check the sense, spelling, and punctuation of your answer and to make sure that no spaces have been left unfilled. It may also jog your memory on an important point which is better tacked on to the end than missed out altogether.

(h) Above all—*practise*. Do not wait until the examination has arrived before you start learning to write against the clock.

Taking examinations

(a) Always read the whole paper right through carefully. The pressure on time always tempts candidates to start writing as soon as they see a question they can answer. Remember, you should aim to select the four questions you can answer best rather than the first four questions you can answer.

(b) Select the questions you know you can answer well. Some candidates attempt questions they have not prepared because they regard them as a challenge. Remember that the examiner cannot know the state of your mind. All he has to go on is the content of what you write.

It is equally important not to pass over a question on the grounds that you know too much about it and could not possibly produce a brief, organized answer. The student who finds himself in this situation has not revised adequately, because revision should include the preparation of 'skeleton' answers for just such an eventuality. Framework essays can be condensed from notes on to a single postcard, to include half a dozen basic points, a possible opening and concluding sentence, a very few relevant dates, statistics, or quotations for illustration, and the names of writers who have displayed a particular interest in the problem under discussion. Writing up cards like these can be a lengthy process, but it is valuable and should not be left until just before the examination. Starting half-way through the course would not be too early.

(c) Attempt as many questions as the paper requires and divide your time between them in roughly equal proportions. You cannot do yourself justice by presenting half a brilliant paper.

R. L. A. Tames

The nature of the British Constitution

What are the most important features of the British Constitution?

The British Constitution is often described as 'unwritten'. It would be more accurate to describe it as 'uncodified'. In Britain, there is no single document which attempts to prescribe all the most important rules relating to the conduct of government. France, Germany, and the USA have written constitutions, but to find out the constitutional position on any particular point in Britain, it may be necessary to consult a variety of sources.

Acts of Parliament, like the Parliament Acts of 1911 and 1949 or the Representation of the People Acts of 1918 and 1948, regulate important matters like the franchise, conduct of elections, and relations between the two Houses of Parliament. Fundamental liberties, the independence of the judiciary, and the succession to the throne are dealt with by the 1689 Bill of Rights and the 1701 Act of Settlement, while there are numerous other important statutes which enshrine customary rights, buttress conventions or commemorate political compromises. Decisions of the courts of law are often significant, particularly in such matters as freedom of the press and interpretations of the law of libel. Basic freedoms of speech and association are implicit principles of the Common Law itself. The law and custom of Parliament, expressed in Standing Orders or 'Erskine May', cover such matters as Parliamentary procedure and privilege. The works of great constitutional authorities, like Blackstone or Bagehot, may also carry weight in a disputed issue. The list of sources is completed by conventions, which constitute an entirely unwritten element and are usually taken as the unique distinguishing feature of the British Constitution. In fact, every constitution, including explicitly written constitutions, like that of the USA, is supported and completed by a mass of conventions. The existence of 'party', the most basic element in the political life of both Britain and the USA is, for instance, purely 'conventional' in both countries.

Conventions are rules of practice; the successful working of the British Constitution depends largely on the observance of these rules. Examples of some of the more important conventions are:
(a) Parliament must meet at least annually.
(b) The Monarch must not attend Cabinet meetings.
(c) The Cabinet is collectively responsible to Parliament on matters of policy.
(d) A Prime Minister who loses the confidence of the Commons must resign or call for a dissolution.
(e) The Prime Minister chooses his Cabinet and acts as its chairman.
Since conventions are not laws, they can be 'broken' without incur-

ring a legal penalty. In fact, as Sir Ivor Jennings pointed out, conventions are rarely ignored because of the practical political difficulties which would follow such action.

As a consequence of its uncodified nature, the British Constitution is generally regarded as 'flexible'. There is no greater sanctity about a law regulating constitutional arrangements than about any other law. Nor is there a special procedure for constitutional amendment, as there is in the USA. A law altering the succession to the throne would be passed in the same manner as a law to establish a National Park. As conventions constantly evolve, this means that the whole Constitution constantly adapts itself to the changing realities of everyday politics.

Britain is a unitary, not a federal, state. There are no regions whose governments have equal status with Parliament, while Parliament has the power to alter or even abolish subordinate bodies like county councils or county boroughs.

Parliamentary sovereignty is recognized by the law courts, which enforce statutes as law and do not presume to pronounce on their constitutionality. No authority in the kingdom is competent to set aside or override the word of Parliament. Parliament can legislate on whatever it chooses and may repeal or amend the Acts of any former Parliament. It can pass *ex post facto* laws and even legalize illegalities, e.g., by granting amnesty to deserters.

The principle of separation of powers does not operate in Britain in the American sense. As Bagehot remarked, the British Constitution is marked by the almost total fusion of its legislative and executive elements. The independence of the judiciary is, however, absolutely respected; judges enjoy considerable immunity of speech and action and are removable only on a joint address from both Houses. In practice, civil servants enjoy a similar seclusion from both the general public and the scrutiny and interference of the Commons.

Explain and illustrate what is meant by the statement that Britain is governed by a unitary constitution.

A unitary state may be defined as one in which there is a single locus of sovereignty. In Britain, this means the Queen-in-Parliament. Parliament is constitutionally supreme. The machinery of local government, for instance, derives its authority solely from Parliament and acts primarily as the agent of central government.

There are, however, regions which enjoy limited degrees of independence, but the derivative nature of their authority implies that there is no federal relationship between the regional authorities and the central government, such as exists in the USA, Canada, or Australia. Northern Ireland sends MPs to Westminster, but has its own Parliament at Stormont and a Governor-General who represents the Crown. Virtually selfgoverning internally in normal circumstances, Ulster's real dependence on Westminster has been revealed by the need to cope with the emergency situation which arose in 1969. The Channel Islands and Isle of Man also retain their own parliaments and are selfgoverning internally, even to the extent of determining their own taxation, but they do not send representatives to Westminster although they acknowledge its legislative supremacy.

Scotland enjoys a considerable degree of administrative devolution. At St Andrew's House, Edinburgh, are the Scottish Departments of Education, Development, Agriculture and Fisheries, Home and Health. As the Scottish Parliament was dissolved by the Act of Union of 1707, Scotland is represented at Westminster. In practice, Scotland is 'over-represented' in terms of strict numerical proportion as a concession to regional sentiment. The resurgence of Scottish Nationalism in the postwar period, however, suggests that further concessions might be necessary, including a regional parliament. Only a few extremists demand separate armed forces and full UN status.

Nevertheless, the Conservative Party in Opposition before 1970 made extensive investigations into the problems of Scotland. In the Commons, there is a Scottish Grand Committee composed of all those MPs representing Scottish constituencies, plus as many other Members as are necessary to secure a reflection of the party balance in the House. This Committee debates the Scottish Estimates, Scottish affairs in general, and the second reading of Bills relating exclusively to Scotland. The Committee Stage of Scottish legislation is taken in a special Standing Committee on which MPs for Scottish constituencies predominate.

Wales has been far more completely integrated with England. The process goes back to the thirteenth-century conquest of Wales. Union was achieved in the sixteenth century. Such devolution as exists has developed mainly since 1945, largely in response to local pressure, resulting from the spasmodic electoral successes of Welsh Nationalists and even from the acts of sabotage performed by the Free Welsh Army.

Although administration is mainly based in Whitehall, there is a Welsh Office in Cardiff. In 1957, the post of Minister of State for Wales was created; in 1964, this was up-graded to Cabinet status. A Welsh Grand Committee and Standing Committee also exist, though they are less powerful than their Scottish counterparts, not least because Wales is only one-quarter the size of Scotland and economically far more closely involved with England.

The theoretical, legal sovereignty of the Westminster Parliament is reinforced by the cultural homogeneity of the British people. Regional loyalties are either vestigial or embryonic; national media, London–dominated, weld the nation together. World wars and the rise of socialism have, in their different ways, almost induced a demand for centralization and uniformity. Extreme opposition to the power of central government is derided, even in the regions themselves. Politically, as well as constitutionally, the United Kingdom Parliament is supreme and unchallenged.

Does the rule of law still exist?

It has recently become fashionable, particularly among lawyers, to argue that the rule of law has been considerably eroded in the present century. Nationalization and the growth of welfare services have necessarily implied increased governmental authority over the rights and liberties of individuals and, more particularly, over their property. Parliament has delegated to Ministers powers to make regulations which cannot be challenged in the courts. Ministries have enormous discretionary powers, but the citizen can appeal to no *droit administratif* of the type that Dicey so confidently derided. The greater use made of administrative tribunals means a large number of bodies or officials making quasi-judicial decisions in a manner quite remote from that of the ordinary courts and equally remote from their jurisdiction. These tendencies, moreover, are increasing rather than diminishing.

This point of view is by no means extreme or even unduly alarmist. There is cause for concern, but these developments must be judged in their proper perspective and they do not, in themselves, imply the elimination of the rule of law. The Executive has great discretionary power, but does not use it in an arbitrary and tyrannical manner. No one is punished except for offences committed and proven by due process of law. As George Orwell remarked, England is the only European country which has never known widespread fear of secret police. The impartiality and authority of the judiciary is acknowledged by governors and governed alike. Government, and its servants, are aware of their responsibility to the people. The Opposition, free press, and common civil liberties exist to furnish the Government with constant reminders of the need to act in accordance with public opinion, a public opinion which has always valued action according to recognized legal procedures and repudiated the arbitrary and unjust. The Crichel Down case of 1954 will be long remembered in

Whitehall. Thanks to the Parliamentary Commissioner for Administration, the Sachsenhausen case has reinforced the practice that departments should interpret the law not according to the letter but according to the spirit if justice is thereby achieved.

Individual liberties do still exist; citizens are free to criticize the government or demonstrate against its policies, and the government will even go so far as to provide facilities and police supervision for these legitimate activities. Liberties have always been exercised within a framework of legal restriction which itself will always give rise to dispute over its extent or over points of detail. Historically, Britain has a creditable record of success in reconciling the desire for social justice with the preservation of individual rights. Ultimately, the rule of law is the expression of the general political values of the British people. There is little evidence that these values have been eroded in the present century.

To what extent does the hereditary principle survive in the British Constitution today and how can its survival be justified?

The devices by which the Crown and the Peers of the Realm once manipulated the Executive and legislature have been swept away by the Reform Acts of the nineteenth century and the growth of a system of competitive entry to the civil service. The Monarchy and the House of Lords still survive, partly by historical inertia, partly on their own merits.

The hereditary element in the House of Lords is at first sight large, comprising more than 700 of its 1100 members. In fact, most of these are 'backwoodsmen' usually granted leave of absence and roused to action, or more usually reaction, only occasionally by a Conservative Opposition wishing to make a forceful demonstration against such measures as the 1969 Transport Bill or the Rhodesian Sanctions Order.

The House of Lords, like Voltaire's God, is so vital to the efficient working of the Constitution that if it did not exist it would be necessary to invent it. Its major function is to revise legislation passed by the overburdened lower House. It also provides a convenient starting point for technical, noncontroversial measures which would otherwise be obliged to wait for time in the Commons. As a debating chamber for topical issues, the Upper House has to some extent been superseded by television. Its judicial functions could be 'hived off', if desired, to a new Supreme Court of Appeal. Its continued existence is guaranteed by the integrity with which it performs the functions assigned to it and the way in which it acknowledges its conventional subordination to the Lower House, providing few occasions for the invocation of the 1911 and 1949 Parliament Acts. The continued existence of the large hereditary element seems similarly guaranteed by the failure of wouldbe reformers to agree on anything but the necessity for reform: powers, composition, selection of members, functions, all are disputed, but no government seems likely to be able to spare enough time and effort to afford the problem due consideration.

The Monarchy cannot strictly be described as purely hereditary as the succession is governed by Parliamentary and, latterly Commonwealth, approval, embodied in the Act of Settlement of 1701 and the Abdication Act of 1936, which together represent a sort of 'elective veto'. The existence of the Monarchy can still be justified in the terms in which Bagehot defended it: it acts as a symbol of unity and permanence, a nonpartisan focus of national loyalty and 'makes government interesting to the masses'. The Monarch, buttressed by the conventional rights to encourage, warn, and be consulted, is in a position to accumulate considerable political experience and act as political counsellor to the government of the day, particularly on foreign and commonwealth affairs, in which a wealth of knowledge has been gained through personal contact. Finally, in the performance of ceremonial functions, the Monarch relieves the Prime Minister while at the same time conferring official approval on the event itself, which may be the result of a socially valuable project, e.g., the opening of a new bridge or hospital, or an important meeting of heads of state to promote mutual understanding and co-operation.

In what senses is Great Britain a democracy?

Edmund Burke defined a free country as one which was regarded as such by its inhabitants. If the same form of definition may be applied to a democracy, then Britain is a democracy. The term certainly requires some definition for democratic theory embraces both the individualism of J. S. Mill and the majoritarianism of J. J. Rousseau. Democracy has, since the American and French revolutions, become the dominant form of government in the modern world. Government *for* the people has become the legitimate principle for authority even in Communist countries. Government *by* the people is rather different and is regarded by the nations of the free world as the major difference between their style of politics and that of the 'people's democracies' of Russia, China, and their satellites. Government by the people implies not direct participation, in the sense of the traditional New England Town Meeting, but rather the presence of democratic institutions by which a law-making body of elected members is made periodically answerable to the electorate.

Britain has all the formal institutions normally associated with a liberal democracy: adult suffrage; regular elections, whose verdicts are unchallenged; more than one political party; freedom of speech, association, and assembly; and a parliament with a 'loyal opposition' with numerous opportunities for questioning the activities of the executive. The free mass media and a multiplicity of pressure groups also remind governments between elections of their ultimate accountability.

There are, on the other hand, a number of features of the British political system which, at first sight, seem difficult to reconcile with Britain's claim to be a democracy. The electoral system has numerous imperfections: unequal constituencies; no provisions for proportional representation; and the selection of candidates by small cliques of party activists. The system discriminates against minority parties, yet only their more ardent members seem concerned that the system should be changed. In both the Monarchy and House of Lords a traditional hereditary element survives, but this anomaly is relieved by the fact that both recognize that they must perform useful, but subordinate, functions, subject to the restraints of convention and constitutional custom which have been imposed on them by the House of Commons. Even the Lords' most daring claim, to act as 'watchdog of the Constitution', rests upon the further qualification that they do so in the name of the electorate. The interrelated factors of class, wealth, education, and occupation impose further limitations on total democratic participation. Members of Parliament are overwhelmingly middle class; senior civil servants are recruited almost exclusively from Oxford and Cambridge; even local councillors tend to be better educated and better off than those who elected them.

Nevertheless, Britain is a democracy because both the people and the politicians think it so. But democracy implies participation and this seems to be greater at the national level than at the local level, with election turnout nearly twice as high for general as for local elections. Even at the national level, there are symptoms which should give rise to concern: the turnout at general elections has been falling steadily since 1959; public opinion polls and Parliamentary candidates report apathy and indifference among voters; 'political' strikes and demonstrations are on the increase and tending to become more violent. This may be a reaction to Britain's economic stagnation and the diminution of her international role and status. Whatever the reason, democracy in Britain must be strengthened by encouraging more participation, perhaps by more education, or by a vigorous intermediate level of regional political activity which would widen the scope for political recruitment and activity and end the enervating division between national and local politics.

Make out a case for the retention of the Monarchy.

The near-absolute power of the Tudor Monarchy has been totally demolished by the demise of the divine-right theory and the rise of representative institutions. Deprived, in practice, of most of her prerogatives, the Monarch continues to exercise political influence; influence which is based, not only on the conventional rights to be consulted, to encourage, and to warn, but on her continuous and varied political experience and on the sincere affection and loyalty of the vast majority of her British subjects.

The erosion of the formal powers of the Monarchy has continued in the twentieth century. It seems unlikely that it will be necessary in future for the Monarch to exercise a decisive choice in the appointment of a Prime Minister. The confused experiences of 1963 led the Conservative Party to adopt a formal electoral procedure for the leadership in 1965. It is equally certain that the Monarch is unlikely ever to refuse a dissolution of Parliament, despite the fact that this Prime Ministerial prerogative has been subject to considerable criticism in recent years. The Monarch does not attempt to interfere with 'her' Speech or the actions of her Ministers, in the name of the 'mandate'. Nevertheless, the Monarch continues to perform functions vital to the stability and wellbeing of the nation: the formalities of approving legislation and instituting governments and parliaments are performed with appropriate dignity; the head of the executive is relieved of many exhausting ceremonial functions, which his abilities and training may not suit him to perform; government is, in Bagehot's words, 'made interesting to the masses'; and the general attachment to a nonpartisan and revered Monarch provides an important stabilizing influence in an age of rapid economic and social change and political uncertainty. This latter function is even more important in relation to the Commonwealth, which has recently endured so many strains that any focus of loyalty and continuity contributes to its continued existence. In addition, the Monarch, and indeed the whole Royal Family, can bestow influential patronage which supports the efforts of a wide range of charitable and educational organizations and campaigns. The experience of King Constantine of the Hellenes does not suggest that a modern monarchy can effectively defend a constitution against revolution, but it can at least deprive the usurpers of the legitimacy they must so desperately seek.

Any case for the replacement of the Monarchy by a presidential system would, therefore, rest upon the production of evidence that the latter would not only perform similar functions to the present Monarchy, but bring additional benefits to justify the fundamental disruption that would be involved in such a change.

'Consultation is the essence of the modern Commonwealth.'   Comment.

The modern Commonwealth has no formal constitution and its members are bound by no all-embracing covenant, but there is an elaborate mechanism for consultation and collaboration in many spheres. The highest level of consultation is at the periodic conferences of Commonwealth Prime Ministers which, until recent times, have normally been held in London. The conferences afford the opportunity for a frank exchange of views, formally and informally, on important issues relating to world as well as Commonwealth affairs. The conference has no executive power, either to enforce resolutions or even to offer its services as a mediator, though it has taken concerted action on specific matters concerned with the 'internal affairs' of the Commonwealth, such as the admission of new members or the 1964 decision to establish a Commonwealth Secretariat. An exceptional, though futile, initiative was taken by the 1965 conference when it established a mediatory peace mission to Vietnam under the leadership of the British Prime Minister. The 1966 conference similarly adopted a positive policy with regard to future action over Rhodesia. These recent instances could be taken as evidence of a tendency for the conference to become a vehicle for action as well as discussion. The main inhibitory factor is, however, failure to agree on joint policies for key issues. Numerous critics have feared that a relentless drive for agreed policies might simply split the conference and itself create fundamental disagreements. This risk is likely to remain with us since the attitudes and objectives of the newer African and Asian members are quite different from those of the old 'white dominions'.

The fundamental purpose of the annual conference, at least until the stormy 1971 session attempted to define purposes and aims, has been to afford members the chance to clarify attitudes and promote understanding in a 'family' atmosphere. Sometimes pressure has been exerted on members to resolve their differences or to influence their policies along agreed lines. The withdrawal of South Africa in 1961 followed condemnation by the conference of her internal administration in terms so strong as to be tantamount to expulsion. But on controversial issues, like British entry to the EEC or future action over South Africa, generally the official communiqué has revealed little more than agreement to differ. Nevertheless, despite differences between what are, after all, sovereign states, their relations with each other are invariably closer than with foreign countries. The regular exchange of confidential news and information is more or less taken for granted and resentment is evident when members feel that the normal channels of communication have been neglected, as over Suez in 1956. The flow of information is carried by the Commonwealth Secretariat, the British Foreign and Commonwealth Office, and the High Commissioners in the respective capitals. Close collaboration also takes place in a number of specific fields, including defence and research. There are numerous standing conferences and committees concerned with such diverse matters as shipping, agriculture, and education, and their efforts are supported by the regular exchange of administrative and technical personnel.

The evolutionary nature of the Commonwealth, its power to absorb new factors and adapt to new situations, has long been regarded as one of its major characteristics. The origin of this evolutionary capacity is to be found in the extensive consultative network which gives advance warning of possible difficulties. It has, for instance, become evident that some African nations believe the Commonwealth to be still exclusively orientated towards Britain and British political objectives. The feeling that it must be seen to belong to all its members was clearly expressed by the President of Zambia when he suggested that Britain herself might be expelled from membership. One motive for the creation of the Commonwealth Secretariat under a Canadian director was the hope that it would contribute towards the desired reorientation. A similar motive lies behind the decision to hold the conferences away from London, in Lagos (1966) and Singapore (1971), under the chairmanship of the Prime Minister of the host nation. If consultation can continue to lead to such successful adaptations of practice and convention, the future of the Commonwealth and its ability to play a significant role in international affairs, seem assured.

What factors would you expect to (a) strengthen and (b) weaken the Commonwealth?

Few formal ties or institutions bind together the member nations of the Commonwealth: common allegiance to the Crown as a symbol of their unity; the exchange of High Commissioners instead of Ambassadors; periodic conferences of Prime Ministers and other Ministers;

the Commonwealth Secretariat; and numerous associations of jurists, educationists, and trade unionists. The 'real' ties which bind member nations together are a common heritage of British rule and its legacies: the English language and legal system; British political values and concepts; cricket and Shakespeare which give rise to a network of cultural and sporting ties. British rule was formerly accompanied by British economic domination: nations of the Empire took British coal, cotton, steel, and gave grain, oil, and rubber, while conducting all these transactions in sterling. A bare vestige of this relationship survives. Commonwealth ties remain: British overseas aid is directed almost exclusively to Commonwealth countries, and is supported by generous aid from Canada; New Zealand still depends on Britain as the main market for her agricultural produce; both trade and aid are supported by technical assistance and emigration in both directions. Cultural contacts remain through Test Matches, Commonwealth Games, Royal Tours, and the Queen's Christmas broadcast.

Military defence pacts still exist between Commonwealth nations and they also continue to show marked constitutional similarities. Nevertheless, powerful forces are simultaneously working in the opposite direction and tending to weaken rather than strengthen Commonwealth ties. The rise of the USA, Japan, and the EEC as major economic powers has disrupted the old pattern of trade and turned Commonwealth nations towards these dynamic economies which, along with Russia and China, compete with Britain in giving aid. In defence, the USA has taken over the leading role and Britain has assumed a subordinate position. Australian and New Zealand troops fight in Vietnam and the ANZUS pact evidently means far more than SEATO. Migration is diminishing and, as a world currency, sterling has taken second place to the dollar. Most significant of all has been the recurrence of major political problems, often conflicts between rich and poor nations, compounded with the explosive issue of race. South Africa was forced to leave the Commonwealth for maintaining her policy of apartheid; India and Pakistan actually went to war with each other; Nigeria has endured a civil war; Rhodesia has successfully defied Britain after UDI; and Australia has modified her immigration policy so that coloured persons are effectively banned. Singapore split off from Malaysia and Pakistan has followed Nigeria in giving birth to a brutal civil war. Even Canada has suffered from the activities of *Quebec Libre* extremists. The Commonwealth Games have been made the occasion of boycotts and demonstrations. Britain's entry into the EEC, even greater political tension in South and East Asia, and attempts at armed insurrection in South Africa, may well finish the process of disintegration which was perhaps inherent in the Commonwealth from the very beginning.

The nature of British politics

How far do regional differences affect British politics?

Of the total British population, 83 per cent live in England, a simple fact which determines that regionalism has very little significance in British political life. The homogeneity of the British people has been remarked upon by numerous investigators and has been attributed to the preponderance of industrial occupations, the large-scale urbanization which accompanies this, and the truly national media which reinforce the uniformity it produces. In Britain, there are no regionally based sectional interests, like peasant farmers, and no significant linguistic divisions. Nevertheless, Scotland, with 9 per cent of the population, Wales, with 5 per cent, and Ulster, with 3 per cent, are ethnically and culturally distinct from England and these differences do have political implications.

Ulster is dominated by its Protestant majority who fear absorption into Catholic Eire and vote in overwhelming numbers for 'Unionist' candidates, who stand for continued association with Britain, and, in effect, represent the local brand of Conservatism. The unique quality of the local situation since 1922 led to the establishment of a local Parliament at Stormont, although national and 'reserved' matters are the prerogative of the Westminster Parliament to which 12 MPs are returned.

Scotland's union with England left her with her own legal, educational, and religious institutions and these have preserved the basis of a separate identity, which, to a limited extent, has expressed itself in resurgent nationalism, fed partly by local economic grievances and partly by restiveness at the remoteness and alleged arrogance of 'London government'. Considerable devolution has taken place in administration. St Andrew's House contains a number of important Ministries, but the local implications of what are seen at Westminster as minor matters, e.g., daylight saving, can produce tensions and frustrations which are not assuaged by the present concessions to national, or regional, sentiment.

Welsh nationalism has also grown from local economic grievances and resentment at Whitehall centralization. Moreover, regional consciousness has been strengthened by the survival of a rich cultural tradition. One Welshman in four still speaks the native language from preference.

These local nationalisms, however, have failed to establish themselves on a mass basis and, despite prodigious efforts by local enthusiasts, have made little electoral headway, except at by-elections, which tend to favour minor parties. Both Scottish and Welsh Nationalists manage to contest about 20 seats at general elections, but whereas *Plaid Cymru* only manages to attract about 8 to 10 per cent of the turnout, the Scottish Nationalists have enjoyed rising electoral successes over the last decade and can reckon to do 50 per cent better than their Welsh counterparts. Other regional political affiliations, like the movement in Cornwall and other minor, mostly Celtic, movements, must be reckoned among the 'fringe' groups which add colour and variety to the British political scene, but little more.

The major parties show some interesting regional variations at general elections. Only once, since the 1945 'landslide', in 1966, did Labour succeed in capturing a majority of seats in England at a general election. Wales, on the other hand, always returns a majority of Labour seats, while the Conservatives have only once won a majority of seats in Scotland in 1955. The Liberals have better success in the South-West and the more remote parts of Scotland, but the fact that they lack a really strong and coherent *regional* basis may help to explain their failure to re-establish themselves as a significant force in national politics.

Homogeneity is the 'norm' of British political culture, but regional consciousness is growing, even within England itself. The dominance of London, which has for so long monopolized governmental, administrative, financial, and cultural functions, is resented and the emergence of the reasoned case for 'regionalism', put by the Royal Commission under Lord Redcliffe-Maud, has created the potential for an institutional framework which could provide positive outlets for these frustrations. Whether regional government would alter the pattern of national politics, by providing a new arena for the growth of minor parties, for instance, as well as promoting participation and more effective environmental planning, it is not possible to predict. It is perhaps for this reason that, Peter Walker reversed the Labour Government's decision to accept most of the Redcliffe-Maud report and settled for a much more modest programme of boundary rationalization.

What part do trade unions play in British politics?

Trade unions are frequently cited as classic examples of 'pressure groups', organized bodies using quasi-political methods to defend or further the interests of their members. Collectively, unions act through the TUC, which consults with Government at Cabinet level and whose co-operation is of paramount importance for the successful implementation of crucial economic measures, like an incomes policy to tackle inflation. Acting individually, unions deal more often with employers, who may in fact be departments of state or public corporations. Consultation and negotiation are the normal procedures, but the strike may be used to force an issue. The inter-relationship of the economy of contemporary Britain enables one group of workers in a key industry almost to paralyze the life of the community. During the first six months of the 1970 Conservative Government, a strike by dockers and a 'go slow' by electricity workers obliged the Cabinet to declare a state of National Emergency on two occasions. It seems possible that in these circumstances the right to strike will be further curtailed by law, as it is in the case of policemen, or else trade unions will lose their peculiar exemption from tort.

Trade unions are far more influential than even their membership of 9 million would suggest, mainly because of their intimate connection with the Labour Party. The original Labour Representation Committee was largely a union creation. The loose term 'Labour Movement' encourages members to think of the political and the industrial as complementary and overlapping rather than distinct and autonomous spheres of action. Unions provide the Labour Party with five-sixths of its funds and many of its local organizers. Naturally, this gives the unions considerable powers of leverage and these are most clearly in evidence at the annual party conference. The conference, is, formally, the ruling body of the Party and the unions' massive 'block vote' makes their support vital for the Parliamentary leadership if it is to maintain its electoral prestige by appearing to run the conference and command unified support. A breakdown of agreement between unions and leadership lay behind the disaster at Scarborough in 1960, when the party leadership's policy on nuclear weapons was rejected by the conference.

Unions do more than provide local party activists and conference delegates, they also sponsor between 120 and 140 MPs. All Labour candidates must be put forward by an organization and unions play an important part in candidate selection even in those constituencies where they are not dominant. In areas like Durham or South Wales, where the old 'staple' industries created strong, local unions, nomination by the union amounts to virtual election. A number of poor constituencies, weak in organization and funds, and facing powerful local Conservative Parties, opt for a candidate from the 'A' roll of Transport House, confident that the sponsoring union will pay up to 80 per cent of the election expenses. As a group, the trade union MPs have usually been stolid and to the right of the party, a steady prop for the leadership except on matters directly threatening union interests. Occasionally, the unions have produced men of outstanding political ability, like Ernest Bevin (Minister of Labour 1940 to 1945, Foreign Secretary 1945 to 1951), or Frank Cousins (Minister of Technology 1964 to 1966), both of whom achieved Cabinet status without first serving a Parliamentary apprenticeship. An interesting new development has been the sponsoring of young 'professionals' like Jeremy Bray and Peter Shore, and this may mark an important departure from previous union policy. Many life peers are also former trade unionists.

The disruptive effects of strikes, fears of Communist influence, and the search for a scapegoat for inflation, have made unions unpopular and, indeed, menacing in the eyes of the electorate, including many who are actually union members. Potential electoral advantage undoubtedly moved Harold Wilson to push his party to the edge of a major crisis over industrial relations in the spring of 1969. The fact that he could carry neither his Cabinet nor, according to Mr Mellish, the Chief Whip, his Commons supporters, with him on this issue shows the power of the unions when faced with a critical issue. Ideological and personal ties with union leaders, the interlinking of the organizations, and the fact that union members are three times more likely to vote Labour than Conservative, all weigh heavily in the minds of the Parliamentary Labour Party and enabled the TUC to win what Peter Jenkins has called 'The Battle of Downing Street'.

Discuss the influence of religion on British politics.

In contemporary Britain, there are few serious religious divisions with the glaring exception of Ulster. Here, religious differences, compounded with serious political differences over the continued existence of the state itself, only serve to emphasize this fact.

Religious controversies had considerable political significance at the beginning of the present century. Until 1922, the presence of a large Irish Catholic group in England and of a disaffected Catholic majority in Southern Ireland was of the utmost importance, bringing the nation to the brink of civil war in 1914. Irish Catholics in England adhered to the Liberal or Labour parties because they favoured Home Rule, while Ulstermen were solidly 'Unionist'. Scarcely less important was nonconformist opposition to the Anglican Church and Conservative Party, which were regarded as almost synonymous. The Conservative Party's Education Act of 1902 gave aid from local rates to voluntary (mostly Anglican) schools. The elections of 1906 and 1910 saw a great deal of discussion of religious issues and direct intervention by Church pressure groups like the Free Church Council and various nonconformist newspapers. The net effect was to cement the alliance between non-Anglicans and the Labour or Liberal parties, particularly in Wales. Although the influence of the Churches has declined rapidly since the First World War, many political leaders of the present generation, particularly on the left, gained their first experience of public speaking, committee work, and organization in Methodist or other chapels.

Religious zeal and observance have declined in most sections of society. There are nearly 30 million nominal Anglicans, but of these only one-third has been confirmed and less than 10 per cent are regular communicants. The Roman Catholic Church claims over 5 million members, but this total includes a large number of children. Nevertheless, attendances at Catholic churches are probably the same as those at Church of England churches. About the same number of people, 3 million, belong to the major nonconformist sects. Probably about 10 per cent of the population attend church regularly. Britain can no longer be called a religious country in the same sense as the USA or most European countries. In education, the role of religion is constantly under attack from a humanist minority, though most people wish their children to continue to receive religious instruction. In practice, such instruction tends increasingly to be moral and social, rather than specifically denominational, in content. The Church has, on the whole, tended to stand aside from political issues, while successive governments have used their power of appointment in such a discreet fashion as to prevent it giving rise to political controversy. However, the Archbishop of Canterbury has taken a firm public stand on the South African arms issue and the bishops in the House of Lords have played a prominent role in debates and legislation on social and moral issues.

To assess the influence of religion in contemporary British politics is difficult in the absence of any major national survey devoted to the subject. In Ulster, it obviously continues to play an important part, elsewhere its role is probably marginal. The old tendency for Catholics and nonconformists to vote left, while Anglicans vote right, seems to have been perpetuated. Local traditions seem to be important in particular constituencies, particularly in areas with large Catholic communities dating from the last century, like Liverpool and Clydeside. A survey of the Cathcart division of Glasgow in 1964 revealed that over 60 per cent of Protestants intended to vote Conservative, while 80 per cent of Catholics intended to vote Labour. Similarly, nonconformity may significantly strengthen Labour in South Wales, while Presbyterianism favours the Conservatives in North-East Scotland. However, it is often difficult to distinguish religious from other factors, like occupation or social status; Catholics in all regions tend to be working class, while practising Anglicans tend to be middle class.

The electoral implications of religious affiliation are, therefore, difficult to assess, but Christian morality continues to exert a powerful effect on the social values which govern discussion of such matters as crime, divorce, education, and censorship. Religious associations are also very active in pressure group politics, either directly, like Toc H, or indirectly, through groups with social or moral aims, like Shelter. At the lower levels of local government, particularly in rural areas where active parish councils survive, the established Church and its rivals may exert influence and provide leadership on a variety of local issues. In national terms, the Church remains far less important than the TUC or the CBI.

'When it comes to politics the man in the street knows little and cares less.'   Comment.

The most searching survey of general political attitudes conducted in recent years was undertaken by Almond and Verba in 1960. Their investigation, published as *The Civic Culture*, covered attitudes in Britain and the USA, and also in West Germany, Italy, and Mexico, thus making it possible to highlight the peculiar features of the British political culture by contrast with that of other nations.

The Briton, to use a category which blurs important distinctions, is more partisan than the average American. Less than half of the British voters have anything positive to say in favour of the opposing party. The strength of party loyalties is a tribute to the national organization of the major parties, the success with which they communicate their programmes and project their image, and the regularity with which loyalties thus created are transmitted by social institutions like the family and the work group.

Like the American, but unlike the Italian or German, the Briton admires and respects his political system, revering it as the product of history and the genius of his nation. Loyalty to the Monarchy is strong. There exists considerable confidence in the impartiality and benevolence of civil servants and the police. Politicians enjoy a somewhat lower status and their pronouncements at elections are regarded with some scepticism.

Most Britons feel free to discuss their politics and believe that they are able to influence the decisions of both national and local government. On the other hand, the average level of political information is low, being closely correlated with length of exposure to formal education. Rose and Mossawir's survey of electoral behaviour in Stockport North revealed that some 40 per cent of voters were unable to give the name of the MP who had held the constituency for 29 years. Most people can identify less than half a dozen major political figures, though the spread of television has probably raised the level of this sort of basic political information, particularly among those who would otherwise be most apathetic toward and ignorant of public affairs. The survey conducted to assist the Mallaby Commission on Local Government revealed considerable general ignorance about the structure and functions of local government. Two years after the establishment of the GLC, a significant minority of Londoners were unaware of any change. Understanding of concepts, like 'devaluation' or the significance of the balance of payments, is still rare, as are the wider political implications of EEC entry. Paradoxically, in the age of mass media, it has become progressively harder for politicians to communicate with ordinary people since the issues have become more technical and complex. Trivialization and simplification seem almost inevitable and the proliferation of slogans and catchphrases, like 'Thirteen Years of Tory Misrule' and 'Labour's Broken Promises', do not suggest that a century of education and rising living standards has yet raised the general level of political debate to the plane of rationality which J. S. Mill hopefully anticipated.

Political knowledge and political participation are not, however, necessarily connected. In terms of some indicators, the level of political participation is high. Turnout at general elections is around 70 to 80 per cent, while 82 per cent of the people questioned in the Stockport survey referred to above affirmed that everyone had a duty to vote. Turnout at local elections is much lower, about 30 to 40 per cent, and the level varies considerably from as low as 8 per cent in some county council elections, to levels nearer that of a general election in large county boroughs dominated by strong local parties.

Membership of voluntary associations encompasses nearly half of the population, but much of this is purely formal membership of trade unions and professional organizations. On the other hand, the number of pressure groups which are influential at a national level was estimated by Anthony Wedgwood Benn at 6000. Their effective direction probably falls into the hands of a self-appointed elite numbering a few score thousands. Membership of political parties includes a quarter of the population but, again, the number of party activists is very low. Probably 1 member in 40 actually participates regularly in political activities. The number of people who could meaningfully be described as 'interested in politics' was reckoned by Almond and Verba at about 15 per cent of the total electorate.

The Briton can, therefore, more accurately be described as a voter, than a citizen. Does his relatively passive role suggest satisfaction with the system or the reverse? A few years ago it was fashionable to say that interest in politics in Britain was dead and even that apathy was a necessary pre-condition for democracy. At present, the situation can be considered less complacently. Turnout at general elections has fallen from 84 per cent in 1950 to just over 70 per cent in 1970. Fewer people are bothering to vote and, among the politically involved, violence and cynical despair have made inroads on the Butskellite consensus. Immigration, inflation, and the EEC have brought British politics alive again in terms of issues. Regional parliaments and a revitalized local government structure could provide the opportunities for a new growth of political participation at the local as well as the national level.

Elections and voting

What are the main disadvantages of the present electoral system?

The most outstanding characteristic of the so-called 'simple majority system' is the unpredictability of the results it produces. In terms of strict numerical proportions of seats to votes, political parties are by no means truly represented in Parliament. The 1951 election presents an extreme example of this, in which the Labour Party gained more votes than the Conservative Party which, having gained the most seats, formed the Government. Many seats are won on a minority vote, in which more votes are polled for candidates other than the successful one. In the 1970 election, 4 constituencies were carried by majorities of less than 100 and 48 by majorities of less than 1000. This situation is most likely to arise when Liberal candidates stand in large numbers, as in 1950, when 187 seats were won on a minority vote. Basically, the system favours the Conservatives. The Labour Party suffers from the large concentrations of Labour supporters in major industrial areas, which means that massive majorities are 'wasted', while the Conservatives, whose support is far more evenly distributed over towns of varying sizes and is strong in the country, pick up more marginal seats. The Liberals suffer too, but for the opposite reason. Their supporters are widely but thinly spread, and they lack firm regional concentrations of support on which to build electoral success. Minor parties are at an even greater disadvantage and likely to be successful only at by-elections, when supporters of the majority parties, knowing that the fate of the Government is not at stake, are more likely to abstain.

A further important consequence of the simple majority system is its 'magnifying' effect. Small shifts in electoral opinion may produce far greater changes in the distribution of seats. If a marginal seat may be defined as one with a majority of less than 5000, then of the 43 such seats that existed in 1951, 77 would have changed hands if 2 per cent of the electorate had voted differently. A 3 per cent swing would have changed 120 seats. The implication is that the 'floaters', whom Nuffield research has shown to be among the least well informed section of the electorate, may in fact decide the outcome of elections.

Opponents of the present system claim that an elector should always be able to make a positive vote and the injustices produced by the lack of correspondence between seats won and votes cast ought to be ended. In defence of the present system, it may be said that it is generally regarded as fair by most of the electorate and there might be widespread suspicion of the more sophisticated proportional systems used on the Continent were they to be introduced in its place.

Moreover, the system does produce a clear majority for one party, thus ensuring that responsibility for government is clearly located, a fundamental pre-requisite of our Parliamentary system.

What forms of proportional representation could be substituted for our present system of voting? Would such a reform be desirable?

Of the many systems of proportional representation which have been devised, the 'alternative vote' would probably be the simplest to introduce into Britain as it is compatible with our present structure of single-member constituencies. Under the alternative vote system, the voter indicates his preference among three or more candidates. If there is no absolute majority of first preferences for any one candidate, the candidate with the lowest number of first preferences is dropped and 'his' second preferences distributed between the other two candidates. Thus, in an average size constituency of 60 000, the following situation might well arise:

A	25 000		A	33 000
B	20 000		B	22 000
C	10 000	(C's second preferences:		
		A 8 000		
		B 2 000		

The major objections to the alternative vote system are that it takes longer to produce a result and the counting of second and even third preferences increases the possibilities of error which could be vital in a closely contested election. Above all, candidates and voters must be confident that the system works efficiently and cannot be manipulated. Without this, general confidence in the value of the whole electoral process may be jeopardized.

A number of proportional representation systems require multi-member constituencies. Under the list system, different parties draw up a list of candidates in order of their selection by the party (some list systems allow the voter to change the order). The party then obtains seats in direct proportion to the number of votes it receives and distributes them to those highest on its list. The single transferable vote system allows the voter to indicate preferences among candidates rather than just vote for a party. Any candidate receiving the required quota of votes (the DROOP quota calculated as: $\frac{\text{Total number of votes cast}}{\text{Number of seats} + 1} + 1$) is elected and his surplus votes are distributed according to second preferences. This process continues until all the seats are filled. The cumulative voting system gives the voter as many votes as there are seats and all may be cast for one candidate, a system which gives a better chance than most to minority parties. All these systems involve more time and expense than the present simple majority system. The second ballot system, by which the whole election is restaged minus the bottom candidate, is even slower and more expensive. Critics of the present system might fairly say, however, that these are not important considerations when set against achieving a fair result at the polls.

There are, however, more profound objections to the introduction of any form of proportional representation. Though it is true that proportional representation gives a more mathematically accurate result than the present procedure, it is doubtful whether it would actually improve the working of the political system. A situation might well emerge in which either the two major parties are so evenly matched that neither can be confident of its majority or else the number of parties might be increased, as in Australia where changes in the voting system led to the emergence of the Country Party and coalition governments. Coalitions are not always weak and unstable; Scandinavia and West Germany have been successfully governed by coalitions. In Britain, however, the efficient working of our Parliamentary institutions is based on the assumption that a strong, coherent, party-based Government will be faced by a strong, coherent, party-based Opposiion. The responsibility for the making and execution of policy is clear and the elector knows when he goes to the polls that his vote is for a Government not a party which must bargain for a share in government.

How would you explain the fact that the Conservative Party attracts one-third of the working class vote?

The phenomenon of the 'workingclass Tory' has an irresistible fascination for students of politics. R. T. Mackenzie has written at length about 'Angels in Marble' and Butler and Stokes have devoted a considerable part of their *Political Change in Britain* to an analysis of the factors which lead so many 'unskilled manual workers' and 'very poor', to vote for the party which most resolutely defends the *status quo*. The 'workingclass Tory' controverts most normal assumptions about British voting behaviour. It seems most probable that no single factor can provide the key to his motivation.

Religion plays very little part in British politics, but communicant members of the Church of England are more likely to vote Conservative than Labour, which continues to draw its strength from the nonconformists particularly in Wales and Scotland. The ultra-Protestantism of Ulster, being compounded with the Unionist issue, provides a peculiar but significant exception to the argument that religion is no longer a significant factor in UK party politics.

The middle aged and the old are more likely to vote Conservative, not altogether because we all become less radical with advancing years, but because, as Butler and Stokes have so convincingly demonstrated, voters are largely creatures of habit, voting as their parents voted, or as they first voted. The middle aged and old of the 1970's had a statistically higher chance of being born in Conservative than Labour households, given the relative strength of the parties. In the long run, it is argued, demographic factors favour the Labour Party. If the election of 1964 had been held with the same electorate as in 1959, for instance, the Conservatives would have won again.

Most women vote Conservative. Indeed, if it had not been for the women's vote, Britain would not have had a Conservative Government since the war. Nor is this a peculiarly British phenomenon; in Europe, both de Gaulle and Adenauer relied on the women's vote, and women are the mainstay of the Christian Democrat and other church-backed parties in Catholic countries like Italy. The tendency of the woman voter to vote Conservative has been explained as the result of her 'innate' lack of radicalism, indifference to public life, low level of formal education, low level of political information, and isolation from influences which might tend to put the Labour point of view, like trade union membership. Trade union members are three times more likely to vote Labour than Conservative and, not surprisingly, strong unions are found most often in the large plants of massive, evidently capitalistic firms, whose very existence emphasizes the division between capital and labour. Women, and other working people who vote Conservative, are more often employed by small 'family' firms, shops, or commercial offices, where trade unionism is nonexistent or at best very weak. The 'revolt' of female telephone operators against their union's strike call in 1971 illustrates this point very well.

'Environment' coincides with and reinforces these factors. Working-class Tories are more often found in predominantly middleclass areas than in predominantly working-class areas, in the suburbs or villages of the South and East rather than in the industrial conurbations of the North and West. Sectional economic interests, like those associated with the presence of a naval dockyard, may also be significant at the local level.

The phenomenon, which Bagehot described as 'deference' a century ago, still survives and exerts a significant stabilizing and neutralizing influence on voting behaviour. Many low-paid workers still believe that the practice of politics is best left to those 'born to it' and educated at the 'right' school. The Conservative Party retains an image of benevolent paternalism and meritocratic competence, while the Labour Party is dismissed by a proportion of its potential supporters as the party of idealists and demagogues. Some Conservative policies, notably on immigration, abuse of welfare services, and strikes, have a strong appeal to large sections of the working class, who feel threatened or endangered and welcome obvious scapegoats like 'coloureds', students, 'scroungers', and Communists. Identification with middleclass interests has also lost Labour many of the votes of the 'rising working class', including a significantly high proportion of women, who self-assign their status above that determined by objective criteria. Intangible cultural factors, therefore, must destroy any complacency which Labour may derive from demographic projections.

How do you account for the low turnout of voters at local elections? What could be done to raise the level of popular interest?

At local elections, turnout very rarely exceeds 40 per cent and may be as low as 10 per cent, particularly in rural areas. It might be argued that this reflects widespread general satisfaction with the *status quo*, but it must be conceded that, even if this is the case, satisfaction is largely founded on ignorance. According to the survey conducted for the Committee on Management of Local Government, 25 per cent of voters are unable to name even one service provided by their local authority. Very few people appear to have regular contact with local government, e.g., through their councillors or by attending council meetings; most rely heavily on their local newspaper for any knowledge they might glean. The survey also revealed that 39 per cent are unable to give any definition of democracy and 36 per cent profess themselves to be quite indifferent about whether they can influence their local council. Three persons in five claim to have voted at the last local election, whereas in fact the turnout was nearer two in five.

The main reasons for not voting at elections appear to be simply lack of interest and the inability to see that local government decisions affect the voter's everyday life which, in turn, can affect the decisions. In addition, among the better informed, there exists the belief that it matters little which party is in office as all the 'real' decisions are taken at a higher level. Another main reason was simple ignorance of the fact that an election was being held. This was particularly prevelant in rural areas where effective publicity demands considerable resources and effort. The weakness of party conflict means many candidates, 70 per cent in some counties, are returned unopposed.

The present situation is unsatisfactory. A healthy democracy demands participation and interest at all levels. Vigorous political conflict at the local level promotes the education of the electorate in public affairs and trains potential recruits for the national arena. Reform of the internal structure of local government, particularly reducing the number of committees and delegating to permanent officials the power to make routine decisions, would leave councillors more time to devote to relations with the public. A real reform of the central government/local government relationship, giving local authorities independent sources of finance, powers of 'general competence', and more discretion over expenditure, would make local government's claim to make decisions that matter a more realistic one. Redrawing of boundaries as such is likely to have little effect on popular consciousness. Closer understanding between local authorities and the public they serve could be fostered by an energetic educational programme, and by enlisting the co-operation of local press and radio, to whom improved facilities should be made available. The circulation of 'White Papers' could promote public discussion on matters of local concern. Finally, it would be a simple matter to arrange to hold *all* local elections, throughout the country, on the same day every three years. This would certainly make it worthwhile for the national news media to concentrate their attention on local campaigning and the general issues involved, leading to greater public awareness, higher voter turnout and, ultimately, more contests and better candidates.

In what ways have the laws governing elections been altered in the last five years? What further changes could be made?

In 1965, a Speaker's Conference on Electoral Law was set up with the purpose of suggesting reforms, particularly with regard to: the minimum age for voting; registration procedure; the possible introduction of preferential voting; the actual conduct of election expenses; and the problems of broadcasting. The case for a lower voting age rested on the higher educational standards among young people, their growing political awareness, and their anomalous position of being able to marry, paying taxes, and being liable for military service, but not being able to vote. Registration procedures had been criticized as slow and inefficient, the electoral roll often being six months out of date and up to 15 per cent of the electorate effectively disfranchised. The Canadian system, whereby electoral rolls are compiled during the electoral campaign, has been suggested as a possible improvement. Computers could also be employed to revise instantly the registers. Preferential voting has long been advocated by supporters of minority parties, but the suggestion has little general appeal and would probably make elections slower and more expensive. Postal voting facilities are currently available to servicemen and Crown servants overseas and their wives, to physically handicapped persons, and to those whose work takes them outside their constituency of registration. Suggestions that the postal vote should be made available to all British subjects living abroad and to persons on holiday have been rejected on the grounds that it would be impossible to collect and count these votes within a reasonable time and it might open up considerable scope for interfering with the secrecy of the ballot.

Investigation and discussion resulted in legislation: the Representation of the People Act (1969) which made a number of important amendments to electoral law, notably the lowering of the voting age to 18, thereby enfranchising some 3 million young persons. Facilities for postal voting were extended to merchant seamen. Limits on Parliamentary and local election expenses were raised to take account of postwar inflation. Broadcasts made about a constituency during the election campaign without the consent of the candidate were made illegal. The names of political parties may now be included on ballot papers. Nonresident qualifications for voting at local elections and the property qualification for elections to a local authority were abolished.

Further reforms that might be considered are: the introduction of proportional representation at local elections, to encourage minorities, raise electoral interest and, hopefully, improve the quality of candidates; the possible use of electronic devices to register and record votes, possibly even from persons abroad or on holiday; the provision of some more effective means of revising constituency boundaries periodically to take account of population changes. The Boundary Commissioners, established by the 1944 Redistribution Act, have had an unhappy history. The spectacle of a government applying a 3 line Whip to its own supporters to vote against boundary revisions it was legally obliged to introduce should be sufficient evidence to convince most people that some satisfactory and respected mode of boundary revision must be evolved.

Parties and pressure groups

Do pressure groups assist or obstruct the working of democratic government?

More than a century ago, Alexis de Tocqueville observed that true democracies, as opposed to nations whose democratic institutions were purely formal, were characterized by the presence of large numbers of 'intermediate organizations' which, he asserted, promoted the flow of political information and particularly controversial ideas; trained men for public life; and prevented too much power from falling into the hands of the state. Nowadays, pressure groups are regarded as natural and necessary intermediaries between government and governed, devices for establishing and articulating the needs and demands of the various social and economic groupings of which society is composed thus facilitating true 'government by consent'.

Pressure groups, of which some 6000 are reckoned to be 'national' in scope and membership, play a vital role in initiating legislation and helping to draft statutes and detailed regulations. Through a network of standing advisory committees, they make available to the departments of state a wealth of expert knowledge and detailed statistical information which it might otherwise be impossible to accumulate. Consultation with affected interests, *via* representative groups, has become a 'constitutional convention' whenever legislation is contemplated. There remains, however, a widespread belief that some groups, particularly the trade unions and 'big business', have too much influence, a feeling which *both* Labour and Conservative supporters respectively share in roughly equal proportions about *both* these 'bogeys'. It is true that producer organizations are stronger than consumer groups, largely because their members' actions can be co-ordinated *via* their work place. The fact that the interests of children, pensioners, and widows are weakly represented seems to be an argument in favour of more pressure groups rather than less. Students, immigrants and, more recently, the disabled and the homeless have shown the way.

Other grounds for legitimate concern are the wealth of some groups, their undemocratic internal structure, and the fact that their Whitehall negotiations are shrouded by a blanket of departmental 'discretion'. These problems could, however, be solved without losing the essential benefits of the present system. Strong Parliamentary select committees could be empowered to make their own discreet investigations into what S. E. Finer has called the 'Anonymous Empire'. There are, moreover, a number of safeguards built in to the present situation. The Government has its own outer defences; pressure groups must show how their interests coincide with the 'public interest'. Cabinet approval must be secured for all major concessions or changes of policy. Regulations made under delegated powers are scrutinized by the Select Committee on Statutory Instruments and all major items of legislation must be consistent with the more or less fixed outlines of the policy and philosophy of the governing party. The groups themselves practise a certain measure of self-restraint and fear to strain relations built up over years with their opposite numbers in government. Above all, it must be remembered that there are so many pressure groups that the greatest restraint on their activity is the competition between them for the attention of the government or general public. Anthony Wedgwood Benn's suggestion that some pressure groups, like Shelter, should be given 'consultative status' within the Labour Party shows, nevertheless, how intimate their relations with government already are.

How does public opinion make itself felt between general elections?

The relationship between an MP and his constituents provides a vital channel of communication between voters and Parliament, but obviously only a very small proportion of the electorate will want or be able to make its feelings and fears known in this way. By-elections offer a similar channel, usually for protest as the votes received by the government party invariably decline, although in only 21 of 243 by-elections between 1945 and 1966 did seats actually change hands. Local elections, too, are increasingly used to register dissatisfaction with government.

The tradition of holding public meetings and demonstrations shows no signs of dying. Massive protests have been mounted on a wide range of specific policy issues, particularly Vietnam, Biafra, and South Africa. It might reasonably be said that students contribute a disproportionate number to these protests, but the presence of over 1.5 million trade unionists in demonstrations against the 1971 Industrial Relations Bill shows that the British people still regard processions and mass meetings as a valid and important method of making their views known.

Mass communications have provided less laborious means of reaching the general public. Letters to the press, interviews and discussions on radio and television reflect current trends of opinion on major issues like EEC entry. Specific opinions on particular policies affecting limited numbers of people are focussed and promoted by a wide range of pressure groups, which not only publicize their own case but, in many cases, enjoy permanent relations with the departments of state and have representatives serving on literally hundreds of standing advisory committees which help to draft legislation or frame regulations. In addition, the appointment of Royal Commissions, Parliamentary Select Committees, and departmental committees afford interested groups the opportunity to put forward their views on an almost infinite range of subjects.

Of all devices, however, none is so straightforward, and perhaps misleading, as the public opinion poll, which since 1937 has informed government and public alike what the 'sovereign electorate' thinks and feels about the most specific and the broadest issues, from the 'breathalyzer' to the general impression of the government's record and competence. It might seem that governments were permanently deafened with the roar of public opinion. Some commentators have attributed the alleged 'immobilism' of modern British governments to an oversensitive reaction to the voice, or rather voices, of the public. Nevertheless, significant sections fail to make themselves heard: the old, the homeless, and the mentally handicapped. Many of those who most need the help of government are least able to demand it.

What is the difference between a political party and a pressure group?

The political party and the pressure group both exist to filter and focus the demands which citizens make on government. They maintain informed positions on the important issues of the day and lend support to governments which meet their demands. In a democracy, where government aims to be responsive to public opinion, pressure groups and political parties are the vital channels of communication between governors and governed.

Parties differ from pressure groups in being primarily political in their aims and methods. Their purpose is the attainment of political office, at the local or national level; their method, the electoral system. Office, as well as being the key to prestige and patronage, gives parties power to implement a wide programme of policies, which reflect the party's ideology or values and its relationship with certain key social and economic groups, like trade unionists or farmers. Attainment of office is the prime aim of political parties, but this involves them in a wider range of social functions: political education, through debate, propaganda, and 'summer schools'; the promotion of social mobility by selecting candidates for office; research, which leads to the development of new policies; and social and recreational activities to confirm allegiances and raise both party funds and morale.

Pressure groups are not primarily organized to gain political office, though they exert considerable political influence over a relatively limited area of public policy: the NFU over agriculture; the TUC over labour legislation; BLESMA over welfare services for the disabled. These are all 'defensive interest' groups, but there are also 'promotional' groups aiming at non-specific membership and the furthering of a particular cause, e.g., the abolition of the death penalty. Pressure groups attempt to influence political decision making by lobbying MPs and organizing publicity and demonstrations. The most powerful and successful groups maintain close, constant, but informal contacts with the departments of state, often by means of a network of advisory committees, and play a significant role in drafting legislation and framing administrative regulations. The fact that pressure groups do not seek to act as the government distinguishes them from political parties.

Some bodies, particularly the minority political parties, do not fall clearly into either category. The Communists and various brands of Nationalists, look and, in some ways, act like political parties. They contest elections and concentrate primarily on political action, but they have little real prospect of attaining office and the vagueness of many of their programmes perhaps betrays their own lack of conviction that they can operate the electoral system to their own advantage. This is reinforced by their recourse to 'direct action' tactics when frustrated in 'pure' politics.

Finally, it is necessary to recognize that parties and pressure groups can never be clearly divided from one another, as they share common personnel and, in some cases, common facilities. Some, like the Fabians, Bow Group, and Monday Club, are 'ginger' groups within the political parties. Others, like the TUC, have organic relations with them. Others, such as the CBI, have no institutional tie, but their influence, on behalf of an interest or a policy, is no less real.

'Mass parties are the creation of mass society.' Comment.

In the mid-nineteenth century, parties were small, leader-orientated Parliamentary groupings with fluctuating power over the political system. Nowadays, parties are massive national organizations with branches in each constituency, conferences attended by thousands of delegates, and a small army of paid agents and research workers.

In many ways, political parties are the most powerful element in modern British politics. The prerequisites for their emergence, an electorate of millions and the secret ballot, which together made traditional informal influences redundant, were the creation of the late nineteenth century. The transition was completed in the present century by the 'nationalization' of our institutions and culture.

In communications, there has been a continuing revolution. The provincial press has withered and lost its political influence. *The Guardian* no longer regards Manchester as its home. National newspapers have become concentrated in the hands of Associated Newspapers, Beaverbrook Newspapers, and the Daily Mirror Group, which, between them control more than 60 per cent of daily circulation. Radio and television have created national news media with the power of instantaneous communication. Telephone and telex services, increased facilities for personal mobility by road, rail, and air, have all reinforced this tendency at a personal level. State education and mass produced goods distributed by chain stores have created a new cultural homogeneity, cemented by the London-dominated media. Cobden's Manchester and Chamberlain's Birmingham no longer retain their cultural autonomy or communal initiative.

Collectivism is now a norm of political action, with state control of social services and education, ownership of fuel and transport, and direction of industrial location and investment. Parties are obliged to think and act in national terms. Perusal of any Parliamentary candidate's election manifesto will reveal how far national issues now preponderate over local ones. The national organization of unions and employers similarly requires that any party with serious pretensions to power should produce national policies and possess a national organization. The further extension of the franchise in 1918, 1928, and 1970 has substantially increased the electorate. The size of the average constituency has now increased to 57 000. Only strong party organizations can conduct successful campaigns in these circumstances and traditional allegiance is itself the major factor in deciding votes at elections. The payment of MPs, which actually began in 1912, permitted candidates without independent means to enter Parliament. At the same time it increased their dependence on party approval for the continuance of their political careers. The independent Member has been eliminated and the Liberal representation in the House reduced to a mere handful. Consequently, the Commons is divided very clearly into Government and Opposition on party lines and any major defeat for the executive is treated as a vote of no confidence. This, in turn, has led to a tightening of party discipline and made party the touchstone of political action and discussion, among both participants and voters. R. T. McKenzie has argued that, in organizational terms at least, the two main parties are in essence identical and, given the nature of our mass society, must be so.

The Member of Parliament

What are the major attractions of an MP's job? Are there any features of backbench life which might discourage potential Parliamentary candidates?

For most Members of Parliament, election to a seat in the House represents the fulfilment of a personal ambition. For leaders, like Edward Heath and Harold Wilson, the ambition was formed and fulfilled early in life; for many company directors and trade unionists, election comes as the conclusion of a successful career outside politics and their stay in the House marks a pleasant prelude to retirement. Few Members, however, fail to seek re-election once they have held a seat and only the aged, the exhausted, and the moribund vacate their places willingly. Whatever the initial motivation to sit in the Commons, it is powerfully reinforced by experience in the House itself. Many Members come to Parliament out of a rather vague desire to 'serve the community' or to be 'in on things'. Some candidates fancy, rightly or wrongly that a place on the backbenches will afford them opportunities for intellectual satisfaction, as well as public prestige, though that may prove a double-sided coin. There are more concrete attractions: a reasonable salary, plus limited allowances towards the costs of a secretary, travel, postage, and telephone calls; five months a year Parliamentary recess: the time and opportunity for part-time employment in, for example, the law or journalism, with the advantage of gaining valuable business contacts. There are opportunities to sit on both standing and select committees, to speak in debates, and to introduce Private Member's Bills. In addition, service in the Commons is the recognized path to ministerial office.

In reality, the life of a backbencher can be tiring, frustrating, and unrewarding. The more conscientious the Member, the more he is likely to suffer. Despite the fact that salaries and attendant allowances have risen four-fold since the Second World War, many MPs, who have no extra sources of income or live at such a distance from Westminster that they must maintain two homes, find themselves with very little cash to spare for legitimate expenditure on travel, study, or research. Little wonder that some Members, though not necessarily the poorer ones, have succumbed to temptation and taken money from, for instance, foreign governments. Facilities in the House are also poor. Few backbench MPs have an office, none has an office to himself, and most are obliged to confer with constituents in corridors or public rooms. Even such elementary items as lockers and telephones are in short supply. Hours are long, up to 14 a day when Parliament is in session, and much of the recess must be spent in the constituency.

Opportunities to initiate action are very limited. Private Members Bills face numerous procedural obstacles and many backbenchers suspect that there may be some truth in the charge that they are mere 'lobby fodder'. J. P. Mackintosh has suggested (*The Government and Politics of Great Britain* 1970) that many MPs seek ministerial office because they are unable to cope with the aimlessness which overtakes many of them on the backbenches. They are, he alleges, grateful to have an office to turn up to and specific tasks to perform, being unable to define their own role satisfactorily for themselves. Party discipline may, of course, make it necessary for a Member to compromise his principles and, more often, eat his words. In practice, Members are rarely forced into crises of conscience. They follow the party line on all but the few issues in which they take a personal interest and they are allowed a free vote on nearly every item of legislation which could be construed as a moral issue. Eating words is rarely painful since the public has long suspected that this is the politician's staple diet.

Many backbenchers must muse that, if events had taken a different turn, they might have been able to earn far more in industry or commerce with considerable security of occupation and a pension to look forward to. An MP's tenure is, in many instances, precarious. The 1970 general election saw many former Members face an uncertain future. There was, however, no shortage of candidates when Quintin Hogg resigned his seat at Marylebone to become Lord Chancellor.

Can a British MP be more accurately described as a representative than as a delegate?

In strictly constitutional terms, it is generally accepted that MPs, once elected, are representatives, free to speak and act according to their own consciences. An MP cannot be forced to resign and is protected by the doctrine that it is a breach of Parliamentary privilege for a group of constituents, or any other body, to seek to limit his freedom of speech. He has, however, been elected on a party platform and owes his seat to the prestige and organization of his party and, in reality, his actions often conform to those of a delegate. Generally speaking, he obeys the party Whip and must bear in mind that to rebel on a major issue is to court disaster at the next election.

A constituency party association can exert considerable influence over an MP's conduct; he may be censured for words or actions and may be called to attend an association meeting to explain his conduct, like Christopher Mayhew for his support of the 1971 Industrial Relations Bill. Few members have the *sang froid* of Duncan Sandys, who rejected the complaint that he did not spend enough time in his constituency, with the reply that he was elected to represent Streatham in Westminster, not Westminster in Streatham. The constituency association, which enjoys almost total autonomy from party headquarters in practice, always retains its 'ultimate deterrent'—refusal to readopt the sitting Member as the official party candidate at the next election. For most MPs this amounts to a political death sentence, though J. M. McKie, Unionist MP for Galloway, and Sir David Robertson, Unionist MP for Caithness and Sutherland, both won their seats as Independent Unionists.

The complaint is often heard that MPs are mere 'lobby fodder' and have fallen far below Burke's noble ideal of the fair minded legislator, unafraid of praise or blame. The case of Nigel Nicolson provides an instructive reminder of the price that can be paid for 'independence'. As MP for the safe Conservative seat of Bournemouth East, Nicolson offended his local party by voting in February 1956, in favour of the abolition of capital punishment and then abstaining, in November of the same year, in a vote of confidence on the Conservative Government's Suez policy. Nicolson refused to give in his resignation when a meeting of local party workers demanded it, and in this he was informally supported by many Members of the House. Conservative Central Office preserved a studious position of neutrality over what it regarded as a dispute which concerned only the MP and the local association. Nicolson showed later, in *People and Parliament*, how the association made it impossible for him to put his case personally to party supporters. He acknowledged the vote of censure passed by a meeting of 400 (out of an electorate of 60 000) but refused to resign and, a year later, was defeated by one vote in 7000 odd in a ballot for the official candidacy. A Labour MP, Stanley Evans, who also abstained on the Suez vote, was similarly censured and did resign. Neither stood again independently, but the experience of Dr Donald Johnson, who was rejected by his local Conservative association for criticizing Harold Macmillan's handling of the Profumo affair, shows that an MP who chooses to stand as an independent against the official party candidate, can split the vote sufficiently to give the seat to the other party, as happened in Carlisle in 1964.

Paradoxically, it is MPs of moderate opinions who are most likely to antagonize their local party, often because party activists tend to hold more extreme views that most of the rank and file, while moderate views can be interpreted as sympathy for the other party. An MP's position is stronger if an election is imminent and if the constituency is marginal, as the local party will wish to preserve its solidarity in these circumstances. If the MP has the support of the national party, he may hope to defeat local discontent, as Major Lloyd

George did at Newcastle in 1951, and the late Mrs Braddock did at Liverpool in 1955. If, however, the conflict arises because the MP fails to acknowledge the party Whip, he has little hope except that the national party will be content to censure him *via* his local party association.

How effectively can MPs exercise control over the actions of government departments?

The scrutiny of government in action has long been regarded as one of the essential functions of a democratic assembly. The effectiveness with which this function is performed depends upon the existence of sanctions which the assembly may apply to an offending executive. In practice, the House of Commons, being divided by strong party loyalties into Government and Opposition, has no capacity for corporate action *vis-à-vis* the government of the day. Not since the 1880s has the House turned out a government and the great days of making and unmaking individual Ministers belong to the 1850s. The sanction of withdrawal of support is now unreal and the methods the Commons now employs are more accurately described as political than constitutional. There are no prescribed pains, penalties, and procedures, but rather a variety of devices which may be turned to the purpose of embarrassing the Government before the electorate. Most of these devices are more powerful when used by MPs acting collectively, rather than individually, or when working in concert with a pressure group or powerful branch of the news media.

Question Time is, doubtless, the most obvious occasion on which the actions of the executive may be brought before the scrutiny of the legislature (this distinction is, in fact, unreal, as Question Time consists largely of Ministers coping with Opposition enquiries). One question and one supplementary scarcely give much opportunity for searching investigation, particularly as the Minister has 48 hours' notice of the question and a staff of civil servants to draw up answers to possible supplementaries. The fact that Ministers answer questions on a rota basis may also mean that a gap of several weeks intervenes between an initial enquiry and a 'follow-up' question, thus depriving the investigation of a momentum and publicity value which is all important. Nor has the MP the advantage of a research team to aid his efforts and put him on a more equal footing with his ministerial adversary.

Adjournment motions and speeches under the ten minute rule may be used to rally public opinion. In practice, major debates on government policy and votes of censure are the prerogative of the Opposition rather than of the individual backbencher.

Backbenchers do have the opportunity of searching enquiries into government activity when acting as members of a House of Commons committee. The Public Accounts Committee does have the assistance of the Comptroller and Auditor-General and his staff of about 500, but the other committees, on estimates, nationalized industries, and statutory instruments, lack such expert aid. All these committees are limited by their confinement to specific spheres of government activity. None is able to investigate any single government department in every aspect of its work.

The Specialized Select Committees set up in 1966 soon ran foul of the practical implications of the doctrine of ministerial responsibility. It was unrealistic to imagine that civil servants would be forthcoming with information that might damage their Minister's standing and it was equally unrealistic to imagine that Ministers would acquiesce in the exercise. In the event, the Committees were given a life of one session and steered away from mainline areas of government activity, like agriculture and education, towards matters of relative indifference to the general public, like Scottish affairs and overseas development. Both Ministers and civil servants returned to their former security, fearing only the unreal threat of withdrawal of Commons support. Even the most startling revelations of ministerial incompetence seem to pass without cries of 'Resign' from *Government* backbenches. Successive Ministers with responsibility for aviation lurch from one financial blunder to another (Ferranti, Hawker-Siddeley, Beagle Aircraft, F-111,—*Concorde?*) with scarcely a rebuke. It is possible that the early demise of the experimental Select Committees was less tragic than might be thought. It is doubtful whether the House would have been able to find time to debate their reports or act on them with any noticeable effect.

The *Ombudsman* offers the best hope of control to Members of the House. His very appointment was a triumph. He hangs like a sword of Damocles over Whitehall. He has already humbled the Foreign Office, but his sphere of influence is greatly curtailed by the fact that complaints about the Health Service, police force, armed forces, local government, and nationalized industries all lie beyond his jurisdiction. For the individual MP, his best course of action is extra-Parliamentary, working with a powerful organized interest, like the AA, NUT, or BMA, or speaking *via* the columns of the daily press or by courtesy of the broadcasting services, self-appointed tribunes of the people.

Upon what sources of information can MPs draw?

Parliamentary democracy implies government by discussion. Effective discussion necessarily depends upon the possession of accurate and adequate information. Where the legislature is denied access to significant information, its influence is greatly weakened. Equally, where its members are overwhelmed by an ocean of data which is largely irrelevant to their purposes the same result is achieved. The House of Commons shows itself liable to both these dangers, but to a limited extent.

On the one hand, there is the alleged veil of 'secrecy' which shrouds not only the deliberations of the Cabinet but also the workings of the various Whitehall departments and, more particularly, their consultations with organized interests. This not only makes the MP a victim of rumour and misinformation, it also contributes to the frustrations inherent in his party-dominated role. Indeed, one of the most important motives behind quitting the backbenches for a junior ministerial post may well be the simple desire to be 'in on things'.

On the other hand, there is the danger of too much information. Barker and Rush recently examined the flow of circulars received by MPs from pressure groups, embassies, etc. (*The MP and his Information* 1970) and concluded that 95 per cent of this material went straight into the rubbish basket without even a glance. This cavalier approach disposes of the problem of unsolicited data, but the ability of most MPs to deal with the complex reports and statistics produced by government departments is very limited and a strong case could be made out for allowing MPs research assistants or even teams of assistants.

Like every other citizen, the MP has access to the media—the press, radio, and TV. Unlike most citizens, he is likely to have extensive, and possibly intimate, contact with reporters, broadcasters, correspondents, and academics, from whom he may glean much information which is invaluable but, on account of the law of libel, unprintable. As the MP, too, often has semi-classified information or knowledge of quasi-official Cabinet leaks, he is in a good position to trade in facts, rumours, and predictions. As the representative of a constituency, an MP will naturally value the media, not for the exclusiveness or novelty of its news content, but because it reflects public taste and interest and thus tells the MP what voters think on matters of current importance and, indeed, what they think *are* matters of current importance. Opinion polls are particularly important in this respect and probably played a crucial role in backbench pressure on Harold Wilson to go to the country in June 1970.

As a Member of the House of Commons, an MP may seek information through Parliamentary Questions. Question Time enjoys traditionally high prestige, though Professor Crick has dismissed it as 'a modest political trip-wire'. Questions can be delayed and re-routed, but they are useful to a backbencher and potentially embarrassing to a Minister. Even if, on matters covered by the blankets of 'National Security' and 'Public Interest', they draw only an informal part-answer in the Smoking Room of the Palace of Westminster, they serve a vital purpose, the more so as Questions are the sole device still wholly in the power of backbenchers.

The MP receives not only his weekly *Hansard* but also the reports of the various committees of the House dealing with public accounts, estimates, statutory instruments, and nationalized industries. There are also the annual reports of the *Ombudsman*, which bring to light such problems as the Sachsenhausen case. The party research departments produce much background material for MPs. Professor Crick has suggested in his *Reform of Parliament* that the Commons Library might well perform a more dynamic role in this respect. J. P. Mackintosh, MP, has put the case for the creation of tough, Specialist Select Committees, appointed by the House itself, with the power to examine the files of government departments, cross-examine permanent officials, and employ independent experts. The experience of the experimental committees, appointed during Richard Crossman's tenure as Leader of the House, suggests that no government is likely to fashion such a strong rod for its own back.

Nevertheless, government does account for much of the information that comes before the MP. White Papers, containing data or policy proposals, are issued periodically, on such matters as defence, or *ad hoc*, on such matters as House of Lords reform. Recently, Green Papers have been published as the basis for public discussion. In addition to the regular publications of the various government departments, there are also the spasmodic but voluminous reports of various Royal Commissions. Although established by government, these bodies have independent members and may pursue a critical line. The reports of other *ad hoc* bodies, like the Scamp enquiry, can also be embarrassing to government. Nevertheless, Downing Street and Whitehall keep a close watch on the flow of information and it remains true that backbenchers were better informed about Britain's involvement in the Crimea in 1854, than they were about Suez in 1956.

Parliament

What, in fact, does the doctrine of the 'sovereignty of Parliament' imply?

The principle of the sovereignty of Parliament is a basic feature of the British Constitution and implies that the Queen-in-Parliament can pass, amend, or repeal laws as it wishes. Parliament can alter the succession to the throne, as in 1936, when George VI became King after the abdication of Edward VIII; it can alter its own powers, as in the Parliament Acts of 1911 and 1949; it can alter the franchise, as in the great Reform Acts of the nineteenth century and the more recent Representation of the People Acts; and it can alter its own composition, e.g., by the creation of Life Peerages as in 1958. Parliament can prolong its own life indefinitely (as in 1939), legalize past illegalities, e.g., by granting amnesty to deserters upon the Queen's Coronation, and make retrospective legislation, as in the case of the Burmah Oil Company. The Constitution knows no doctrine of judicial review and no court has the power to declare a statute unconstitutional, though Parliament may set aside the verdict of a court. Parliament has successfully asserted its supremacy over both the Royal Prerogative and the pretensions of the Common Law judges.

Theoretically, Parliament is supreme; in practice, its actions are subject to very real limitations. Treaties, conventions, protocols, and other obligations of international law restrain the political power of Parliament. Britain's adherence to the Universal Declaration of Human Rights, membership of the UN and the Council of Europe, of NATO and the Commonwealth, all impose restrictions, none of which may be intolerable in practice, but which exist none the less. No change in the succession to the throne or in the Royal Style and Titles can be made without the consent of all members of the Commonwealth. Since the 1931 Statute of Westminster, no law made by the British Parliament extends to any member of the Commonwealth except at its request. Entry to the EEC might well imply more fundamental changes and could eliminate the concept of sovereignty altogether. As it is, Britain's political and economic dependence on the USA (witness Suez as evidence of the one and deflationary fiscal policies as evidence of the other) make the reality of sovereignty rather dubious anyway.

Parliament, or at least the Commons, is elected. Even their Lordships recognize their role as servants of the public and presume to obstruct the Lower House only when acting in that capacity. Electoral approval of major legislation sometimes couched in the vague concept of 'the mandate' is, therefore, a fundamental assumption of practical politics, partly because effective laws really do rest on consent. The existence of a free press and a multiplicity of organized interests ensure that Parliament remains responsive to opinion throughout its life and consultation with affected parties, often *via* statutory departmental committees, has become an important 'convention' of the Constitution.

No limitation of Parliament's supremacy is more real than that imposed by the Government of the day, which now controls the time, procedure, and actions of the Commons. The Government initiates almost all major legislation and only refers to Parliament's 'sovereign' law making status to circumvent difficult political issues, more or less forcing backbenchers to vote 'freely' as 'sovereign legislators' on issues, like the abolition of capial punishment, which, in fact, have the informal support of the Cabinet. Likewise, governmental control of finance is almost unchallenged; a situation which party discipline upholds. The real function of Parliament is not to make legislation but to criticize or approve the actions of Government. Even the performance of these limited functions is largely in the hands of the dominant party. As J. P. Mackintosh emphasizes (*The Government and Politics of Great Britain*) this will remain the case until the electorate wishes it otherwise.

'The procedure of the House of Commons is now a positive hindrance to good government.' How could the procedure be improved?

The Commons has two main functions: legislation and the scrutiny of government policy. In the performance of these tasks, it is impeded by the outmoded rules and conventions which regulate its procedure. Devices like 'Supply Days' or the rejection of bills by the formula that they be read again six months hence, are more than quaint survivals, symbolizing the great traditions of the House; in practice, these anachronisms may constitute a grave impediment to the proper performance of the necessary functions of a democratic assembly. The procedure of the House has simply not developed rapidly enough to keep pace with the extension of government activity in welfare, education, and industry or to cope with the enormous volume of legislation necessitated by this enlarged role. Institutions have a conservatism of their own, which they appear to pass on to their members. Where respect for tradition, simply because it is tradition, is strong, this effect is doubly reinforced. The atmosphere' of 'the best club in London', which so powerfully affects new Members, may prevent the Commons from becoming little more than an antechamber to the 'corridors of power'. Between the Balfour reforms at the turn of the century and the Crossman initiatives after 1966, procedure was left to develop by the process which critics of the House call 'muddling through' and defenders christen 'evolution'.

There is no lack of reforms which the House might put into action; rather it is time and initiative that are lacking. Since the House has lost its corporate existence and is largely dominated by the Cabinet, procedural reform must wait upon a government which is either unselfish with Parliamentary time or else appreciative of the long-term dangers implied by continued neglect of procedural reforms. Some important steps have already been taken. There is now less legislation by the Whole House, but even more use could be made of committees in order to reduce this cumbersome device still further. A Second Reading Committee has been established to deal with this stage of uncontroversial legislation. The procedure on the Finance Bill has been remodelled to allow most of the details to be dealt with 'upstairs', in committee, leaving the Opposition a few choice items to toy with on the floor of the House.

An attempt was made to lengthen the time available by introducing morning sittings, but this was unpopular with MPs who needed the time to attend to legal practices or other employment, or else found it impossible to keep up with other Parliamentary commitments. The experiment was, therefore, brought to a premature conclusion. It has been suggested that sessions might be lengthened beyond their present seven months, but such a step would meet opposition from both Ministers, who begrudge time spent away from their departments, and backbenchers, who use the recesses for study, research, constituency work, or casual employment in the law, commerce, or the mass media. It should not, however, be impossible to devise a method of carrying over uncompleted bills from one session to the next, particularly Private Member Bills, which endure so many procedural frustrations at present. In 1964, the Select Committee on Procedure criticized the waste of man hours involved in the physical act of voting and proposed the introduction of American-style electronic devices. Needless to say, this revolutionary proposal was dismissed with indignation and contempt. There is hope in the fact that the Select Committee on Procedure is now a permanent body, keeping procedure constantly under review, and able to accumulate both expertise and prestige, rather than an *ad hoc* body appointed every decade or so.

Effective procedural reform depends upon a realistic appraisal of the power and potential of the House. Most legislation is government legislation and, given the strength of current party discipline, unlikely to be rejected. The main legislative role of the Commons is, therefore, detailed amendment, for which it should command the most expert knowledge available. The present system of large unspecialized standing committees could be replaced relatively easily by an increased number of specialized committees, with about 15 instead of 40 members. It should also be part of the Commons function to follow up legislation and assess its value in action. The function of scrutiny could be extended by allowing more time for Questions, and more supplementaries, though this could only be achieved by encroaching on other parts of the timetable. Specialized Select Committees, with the power to investigate the work of government departments, employ expert advisers, and interrogate civil servants, have long been a favourite proposal of reformers like Professors Crick and Mackintosh. The experience of the experimental committees on Agriculture and Education, appointed during the Crossman regime, suggests that no government would be willing to make such a strong rod for its own back. The Parliamentary Commissioner, barred from investigating complaints regarding the police force, health services, local government, and nationalized industries, represents the extent of 'permissiveness' on the part of government. Procedural reform, which fails to take account of the real powers and intentions of modern Cabinet governments, will be worse than useless. It will be illusory.

Discuss the role of the party Whips in Parliamentary government.

The Whips are often cast as the villains of the Parliamentary pantomime, obedient servants of a power-crazed executive, exacting the reluctant obedience of MPs broken in spirit and ravaged in conscience. The very word 'Whip' has sadistic connotations and it is tempting to identify the activities of these party 'thugs' as the long lost 'cause' of the 'decline of Parliament'. In fact, the Whips do more to help than hinder good government and their activities are the expression of party discipline, rather than its origin. Party discipline exists because the electorate will have it so. The case of Nigel Nicolson, MP for Bournemouth East at the time of the Suez Crisis, shows how a constituency association will go beyond even the appointed officers of its Parliamentary party in its demands for loyalty. Only one MP since the Second World War has been re-elected by his constituency after the Whip was withdrawn from him. Even in local elections, where independents might be expected to do better, they in fact come off consistently worse than the candidates of the major parties.

The disciplinary functions of the Whips naturally attract the attention of the press, eager to side with or villify 'rebels', to speculate on their likely 'punishment', and to gloat over the discomfiture of the party. The organizational functions of the Whips, being more mundane, attract almost no attention from the press, although they are vital for the efficient running of the House: 'pairing', the manning of legislative committees, and the ordering of the Parliamentary timetable do not arrange themselves. By keeping MPs informed of the forthcoming business of the House, Whips help to make Parliament more, rather than less, effective than it might be otherwise.

The Whips are the main channel of communication between the party leadership and its supporters on the backbenches. From the top flows information and reassurances; to the top comes the current of backbench feeling. The decisive turning point in the struggle to introduce a Trade Disputes Act in 1969 was the announcement by Mr Mellish to the Cabinet that he could not guarantee backbench support for the Bill in the House. By acting as channels of communication, the Whips serve the patronage system. It is they who note the names of MPs assiduous in the unglamorous task of committee work; rewards of office and honour are distributed accordingly. The key role of the Whips as the eyes and ears of the party leaders is reflected in the fact that the Chief Whip's office is at Number 12 Downing Street, next to the two senior Lords of the Treasury. Nor is it without significance that Edward Heath attained his high office *via* the ranks of assistant and later Chief Whip (1955-9) holding the party together through the difficult post-Suez period and, at the same time, building up an unrivalled knowledge of the working of the party machine.

What is the role of the Opposition in the British political system?

British Parliamentary democracy is based on the recognition that the nation contains groups with opposing points of view on major public issues. Whereas the American Constitution places external checks upon the power of the government of the day to make decisions, in the British system the check is primarily internal, the existence of a recognized 'Loyal' Opposition in the House of Commons. This Opposition is characterized by its permanence and by its degree of organization, with a recognized Leader, salaried as a Minister of the Crown, and a communications system of Whips and backbench committees. It is, moreover, representative, having an organic connection with a group of party followers organized on a nationwide basis.

The constitutional functions of the Opposition are to participate in the deliberations of the Commons, both on the floor and in Committee, and to oppose government policies by voice and vote, seeking to modify where it cannot reject, in the name of general and special interests. This strict account of the role of the Opposition would, however, be misleading if taken at face value. The Opposition is based on a united political party which seeks to gain office and uses the arena of Parliament to stage a continuous electoral campaign. By manning the various standing committees, the Opposition assists in making essential legislation and by providing chairmen for such key committees as those dealing with public accounts and statutory instruments, the Opposition contributes to the role of Parliament as the watchdog of the executive. Nevertheless, the main aim of the Opposition is to propose an alternative programme and to present itself to the electorate as a credible alternative government. The knowledge that Government and Opposition may reasonably expect to exchange places in the foreseeable future obliges both to some extent to moderate their criticisms of each other and their promises to the electorate.

The effect of this is to reinforce the existing political consensus to the point perhaps where electors can sometimes claim to see no difference between the parties, who continuously bid against each other for support at the polls. The mere fact that the Opposition makes an encouraging gesture towards pensioners or farmers, and meets with a good response, obliges the Government to counter or outbid such moves. Comparison of party manifestos reveals much common ground between the parties, emphasis on housing, education, and social services, for instance, or, more recently, a positive policy towards environmental control. Both parties are in favour of EEC entry, and neither advocates withdrawal from NATO. To some extent campaigns must, therefore, be couched in language which encourages committed supporters without alienating potential 'converts'. In an age of 'Butskellism', as R. H. S. Crossman remarked, the one thing the parties cannot do without is their myths, for on so many issues that is all there is to distinguish between them, except their vociferous claims to a virtual monopoly of political talent. Thus Edward Heath had to shout for 'Free Enterprise' while effectively nationalizing Rolls-Royce.

The fact remains, however, that party discipline is now so strong that the Opposition cannot expect to defeat the Government in a floor vote and force it from office. This has not happened since 1895. The most it could hope for would be government abstentions of such proportions as to discredit the policies and ability of the administration in the eyes of the electorate. Even then, the Opposition would have to wait until the next election to gain office. The recovery of the Conservative Party after the 1956 Suez crisis suggests that such a possibility is remote. Even after the long leadership crisis of 1963, the Conservatives only lost the 1964 election by a very narrow margin. The resignation of Chamberlain in 1940 was quite exceptional and even on that occasion the Conservative Government managed to win the vote over the handling of the Norwegian campaign by 81 votes. In normal circumstances, an Opposition may reasonably hope to do three things: wring legislative amendments from Government, particularly when supported by important outside interests; expose the weakness or injustice of government policies, which may lead to amendment of executive decisions, again if supported by outside pressures; aspire to win the allegiance of substantial numbers of voters. Speeches never win votes inside the House, but they are aimed at a larger audience and serve as a constant reminder to Government that its power is limited and contingent upon the assent of the electorate.

Discuss the cases for and against televising debates from the House of Commons.

It might seem anachronistic that in an age of instantaneous, electronic mass communication, the British still rely on the old fashioned lobby correspondent to bring them reports of Commons debates at second hand. The House jealously guards its privacy and even restricts the number of places available for 'strangers' who wish to watch its proceedings in person. It is plainly impossible for any sizable proportion of the population to do even this. Thus the televising of Commons debates seems at first sight to offer numerous advantages. Enthusiasts for the project have advanced some interesting arguments in its favour. Television would enable the voter to attain a new sense of political reality and increase his knowledge of public affairs, thus enabling Parliament to perform what Bagehot emphasized as its educative function, vital for the continued development of a true democracy. It would, in a sense, promote 'participation', diminish apathy, and generally re-invigorate faith in the traditional political system at a time when it seems threatened by the discontents of strikers and demonstrators and the machinations of remote bureaucrats. More than this, televising Commons debates might rejuvenate the House itself, make discussion lively and meaningful, and put an end to dull set-piece speeches delivered to an empty chamber. It would also restore the confidence of the backbencher in the value of his constitutional role.

The potential value of television *is* incalculable, which is precisely why it will continue to be excluded from the Commons. To televise debates would raise far more problems than it is likely to solve. Unless one were prepared to broadcast all debates endlessly, editing would be necessary and in itself this would pose great problems of responsibility and judgement. Television might, moreover, favour, to an even greater extent than debate already does, those MPs whose talents are oratorical rather than administrative. The results may be imagined: even more antics from some of the more colourful 'characters' on the backbenches and pressure on every Member to say something so that his constituents may be assured of his assiduous attendance to their interests. Committee work and the other routine aspects of the Commons daily round might well suffer from a lack of volunteers for unpaid, unglamorous, and un-televised proceedings. Even debates can scarcely be regarded as good television material with intrinsic viewer interest. Few people would wish to see anything other than the State Opening and the Budget Speech; though some might enjoy Question Time. Televising Commons debates alone would give a totally misleading impression to the viewer of how legislation is actually made and government policies scrutinized. As the House itself voted against even an experimental period of televising in 1966, and its control of its own affairs is undisputed, the debate on the merits of this step is likely to remain academic. On the other hand, the Upper House has expressed more than a passing interest in the possibility and here television could offer numerous advantages and would raise fewer apparently insurmountable problems.

What are the prospects for the reform of the House of Lords?

The preamble to the 1911 Parliament Act announced that the statute, while fundamentally altering the relationship between the two Houses of Parliament, was a purely temporary measure, pending some larger and more permanent constitutional adjustment. Sixty years later, the cause of reform still languishes. Their Lordships have done little to provoke the Commons, except perhaps in the years 1929 to 1931. Since the Commons has for the most part been preoccupied with war or controlled by the Conservative Party, no major constitutional crisis has arisen, as it did in 1909, to provide the occasion for sweeping measures of reform. An all party conference broke down over the question of the powers of the reformed House in 1948. The Parliament Act of 1949, the introduction of Life Peerages in 1958, and the Peerage Act of 1963, represent no more than limited tinkerings with the powers and composition of the Upper House-the 1949 Act to get steel nationalization through, the 1963 Act to resolve the Wedgwood Benn impasse. The introduction of Life Peerages has had a beneficial effect on the House and given it a major injection of new talent and expertise. It could be argued, however, that by enabling the House to carry on in its present form, it has merely helped to postpone inevitable and necessary restructuring.

Harold Wilson's attempt to reform the Upper House was scarcely more premeditated than previous legislation affecting the Lords and arose from a purely political situation. Stung by the rejection, albeit purely symbolic, of the Rhodesia Sanctions Order, Mr Wilson abruptly curtailed the all party talks on Lords reform and a White Paper was hurriedly published, outlining the Government's proposals. The reformed House would be a two-tier structure comprizing voting peers, who would be life peers or first holders of a title, and non-voting peers, with the right to speak and serve on committees. The composition of the House would be arranged to include appropriate numbers of peers from Scotland, Wales, and Ulster, and the regions of England. The House would have a six-month delaying power on ordinary bills, but no powers of final rejection. Law Lords and Bishops would continue to sit in the Lords and all peers would be qualified to vote at Parliamentary elections. The strength of the voting House would initially be about 230 and arranged to give the Government a small majority over the opposition parties but not over the House as a whole, 'cross benchers' holding the balance. Most of the White Paper's proposals were introduced as a draft Bill in 1969, but were dropped in the face of determined procedural opposition by an unholy alliance of right-wing Conservatives and left-wing Socialists, the former objecting because the Bill went too far, the latter because it did not go far enough. Having temporarily lost control of the Parliamentary timetable through bad management and worse judgement, the Government was obliged to drop the Bill entirely from lack of time in order to make way for a more urgent, and even more controversial, industrial relations bill.

The 1969 Bill had many imperfections, notably the concentration of great powers of appointment in the hands of the Prime Minister, but it was a step towards abolishing the anomalous hereditary backwoodsmen and strengthening the efficiency and prestige of the Upper House. Reform is fraught with problems: the composition of the House, the manner of its election, its powers, and its responsibilities. Reformers are broadly divided between those, mainly Conservatives and lawyers, who want it to play the role of constitutional watchdog, and those, mostly Socialists and political scientists, who want it to act as maid-of-all-work to the Commons, attending, in Professor Crick's words, to what the Commons has left undone rather than presuming to censure what it has done. The existence of these divisions and differences perpetuates the life of the present structure and it is evident that reform is unlikely in the near future, unless some unforeseen crisis emerges. Since Government is hard pressed to find time for the legislation it must deal with, it is unlikely to tackle the thorny problem of Lords Reform unless it is obliged to by circumstances.

The changes that may take place are likely to be evolutionary and gradual, sanctioned and supported by convention rather than imposed by statute—an increasingly dominant role for Life Peers and perhaps the growth of joint committee work by members of both Houses. Major reform seems condemned to remain the subject of academic discussion.

What privileges does Parliament possess and why?

Both Houses of Parliament claim the right to 'ancient and undoubted' privileges which do not arise from statute or permission of the courts. Claimed at the opening of a Parliament, these privileges are upheld by Parliament itself, but cannot be extended. Their purpose is not to give a Member special immunity from the law, but to allow him to perform his duties without hindrance. When an MP was arrested for speeding, for instance, his plea that he was hurrying to an important division was not accepted by the courts as a valid claim to privilege.

The most basic privilege is freedom of speech, first asserted in Eliot's Case (1629) and upheld in the Bill of Rights (1688) which allows Members to speak in Parliament without fear of action for libel in the courts. Members must be free to speak openly in the public interest, but a Member who abused this privilege to defame an individual or organization unjustly would surely be penalized *politically* by the press and possibly by his party.

The House has the right to regulate its own behaviour and the power to enforce its own rules. Bradlaugh, the nineteenth century atheist, for instance, was barred from taking his place in the House because, although duly elected, he refused to take the oath. The obstruction caused by Irish MPs to draw attention to the Nationalist cause led to the introduction of devices to control discussion: the closure, guillotine, and kangaroo. Rules of behaviour are strictly observed; MPs cannot refer to each other by name, must address their remarks *via* the Speaker, may not speak insultingly of either House, or use the name of the Sovereign either slightly or for the purpose of influencing the House. Breaches of Parliamentary etiquette may be disciplined by reprimand or, in extreme cases, expulsion. 'Strangers' within the House, or outsiders beyond its walls, e.g., journalists, may be committed for 'Contempt of the High Court of Parliament'. Strangers may be ordered to withdraw from the public galleries if the House desires to receive information in secret, as it may do in time of war or national emergency.

Parliamentary proceedings have a right to publication, primarily in *Hansard*, while a newspaper giving an accurate account of a debate cannot be sued for libel. In 1966, the House, on a free vote, rejected a proposal to televise its proceedings for a trial period.

Some of the more ancient privileges of the House are now, in practice, redundant. Few MPs are likely to evade arrest for debt and the impeachment of Ministers has been abandoned for 150 years. The House of Lords continues to act as a final court of appeal and may settle disputed peerage claims, but no peer now takes advantage of his rights to give advice to the Sovereign, vote by proxy, or refuse to attend court when served with a *subpoena*.

Why is the office of Speaker so important?

The Speaker ranks as first commoner in the land on ceremonial occasions; he represents the House and, more important, plays a vital part in its smooth running. Elected at every new Parliament, by a vote which is normally unanimous, he is invariably re-elected for as long as he wishes. The election of a successor to Dr Horace King, the first Speaker to come from the Labour Party, led to disorderly scenes in the House as backbenchers objected to the manner of the Speaker's selection, which they regarded as a 'deal' between the Government and Shadow Cabinet from which they were excluded. They, at least, were able to register a protest; not so the Speaker's constituents, who are deprived by his election of the services of their MP. Convention decrees that he shall be returned unopposed by candidates of the major parties and his constituency functions shall be shared among MPs for neighbouring constituencies. It has been suggested that he should sit for a specially created seat to be known as St Stephen's, Westminster. The Speaker receives a salary equal to that of a Cabinet Minister and is entitled on retirement to a peerage and a pension. Dr King's pension also became the subject of controversy as Labour backbenchers opposed it to attract publicity to their protests against government economic policies and their alleged effect on wages.

The Speaker's main task is to supervise debates in the Chamber. He must maintain order, check delaying tactics, warn Members against repetition and obstruction, and interpret the complex rules and standing orders of the House, in which he is assisted by a Clerk. His very presence acts as a constant reminder to Members of the procedures which it is his duty to enforce. Members wishing to speak must 'catch the Speaker's eye'. The Speaker has usually prepared for his own use a list of potential speakers to whom priority is to be given. This would naturally include Ministers and frontbench spokesmen concerned with particular issues, but in a debate on the coal industry, for example, would recognize the claim of Members representing South Wales and Durham, while a debate on fishing would mean the inclusion of the Members for Hull and Grimsby. The Speaker must also apportion time between Government and Opposition and set aside a fair time, often a disproportionate amount of time, for those who represent minority or unorthodox viewpoints.

The subsidiary duties of Mr Speaker are very varied and include: deciding what is a Money Bill, within the terms of the 1911 Parliament Act; deciding who is to be regarded as official Leader of the Opposition (usually a formality, but governed by the Ministers of the Crown Act, 1937); appointing a panel of MPs at the beginning of Parliament, from whom he chooses the chairmen of standing committees; allocating bills to standing committees for their 'committee stage'; deciding whether a motion of 'urgent public importance' is justified. As the official representative of the House, his original office, he claims its privileges from the Sovereign and also executes its orders regarding, for instance, the suspension or expulsion of Members, or the punishment of outsiders for contempt. His most everyday task is to supervise divisions and to pronounce their result. In the rare event of a tie, he may cast a deciding vote.

The job of Speaker is a demanding one and the election of a new Speaker presents many problems. Candidates must obviously have considerable experience of the House, but must be prepared to renounce further political ambitions and act as the non-partisan figure whose decisions will be accepted without question. Personal qualities of tact, dignity, and humour are naturally invaluable for such a role, but the existence of the clerks and other officials of the House probably validates the old dictum that 'all Speakers make good Speakers'.

Central government

What were the main findings and recommendations of the Fulton Report?

The Fulton Committee was appointed in 1966 to examine the structure, recruitment, management, and training of the home civil service. Being composed of academics, businessmen, former civil servants, and MPs, it was able to draw on expert knowledge. Besides receiving the views of hundreds of witnesses, it also took into account the results of a number of specially commissioned research projects and a report from an organization of management consultants.

The tone of the committee's report was critical. It accused the service of clinging to the philosophy and practices of the Northcote-Trevelyan Report and thus of failing to come to terms with the problems of a complex and rapidly changing technological society. Specific charges were that: the service still placed too high a valuation on the capacity of the gifted amateur; the system of 'classes' impeded the best use of available personnel; the specialist classes were denied adequate opportunities to exercise administrative responsibility; knowledge of modern management techniques was generally inadequate; the service was too isolated from the community it was supposed to serve; and that training and career planning, officially the responsibility of the Treasury, were inadequate.

The proposals the report put forward to remedy these defects were equally trenchant. A new Civil Service Department, responsible to the Prime Minister, should be set up to replace the Civil Service Commission and the Pay and Management sections of the Treasury. The new department's main responsibilities would be recruitment, personnel training and promotion, and the diffusion of such skills as 'O and M' and knowledge of computer applications. All classes should be abolished in favour of a single grading structure, thus facilitating flexible career development, speeding promotions, and ending harmful distinctions between specialists and generalists. A Civil Service College should be set up to conduct appropriate training and research programmes. Recruitment policies should allow more late entry and encourage the interchange of personnel with private enterprise, nationalized industries, and local government. As far as possible, the principle of 'accountable management' should be applied to the work of departments and its implementation would be assisted by the establishment of planning units and senior policy advisers to assist Ministers. 'Hiving off' semi-autonomous units was also approved.

'Fulton' has had its share of criticism too, notably from Professors Griffith and Robson. The report, it is alleged, has a number of major defects: failure to define precisely what *is* meant by 'professionalism'; failure to examine the relationship between civil servants and Ministers; failure to appreciate that administration and management are not the same; and failure to ask the most basic question—what is the proper function of the civil service? It is no use saying 'look at the job' if the 'job' is left undefined. Once functions are clear an appropriate structure can emerge easily. The report has, moreover, been attacked for its carping tone and caricature presentation of the service as it stands. Nevertheless, many of its recommendations have been effected; a Civil Service College is now in being and a start has been made on the abolition of the system of classes. In other words, where the report coincides with trends already emerging from the service, it has been implemented, where it conflicts with it on fundamentals, as in the creation of senior policy advisers, it has made little progress.

What are the responsibilities of a British Prime Minister?

The press has made much of the difference in 'style' between the premiership of Edward Heath and that of Harold Wilson, a difference which the two party leaders emphasize for the sake of their electoral images. This emphasis seemingly bears out the much quoted aphorism that the office of Prime Minister is what the holder chooses to make of it. While the office is conventional, however, it would be misleading to think of it as infinitely flexible. If the Cabinet is the keystone to the arch of the Constitution, then the Prime Minister is the keystone to the arch of the Cabinet, and his failure to perform a fairly extensive range of functions would necessitate a fundamental readjustment in the working of the whole Constitution. A brief survey of the premier's many functions will reveal how pervasive is his influence, how pivotal his role as co-ordinator and leader.

Once invited to form a government, it is up to the Prime Minister to choose not only the members of his Cabinet but also to select occupants for a hundred other lesser offices. His freedom of choice will necessarily be limited by the human resources available to him and the political debts he must pay, but the choice is still his. In office, his powers of appointment extend to Lords of Appeal, Bishops and Deans of the Established Church, Privy Councillors, and Peers. He advises on the distribution of Honours, is consulted on the appointment of Governors-General, and approves the promotions of senior civil servants of the administrative grade. Since the acceptance of the recommendations of the Fulton Report, he has been officially, as well as *de facto*, head of the civil service.

As chairman of his selected Cabinet, the Prime Minister convenes the Cabinet, controls its agenda, settles disputes between its members, and summarizes the sense of the meeting. He acts as its official spokesman in public and it is to the premier that the Cabinet secretariat is, in practice, largely responsible. In the absence of the premier, the Cabinet functions imperfectly. Lord Morrison's graphic account of his attempts to deputize for the absent Attlee shows how the effective functioning of the Cabinet depends on the existence of its leading member, whose so-called 'presidential' style of government has been supposed, by Lord George-Brown, Humphrey Berkeley, and others, to have superseded Cabinet government itself.

As leader of the governing party, the Prime Minister is expected to take a personal lead on all major policy issues and to put forward his views in the House and on television. The standing of the Government as a whole depends largely on the standing of the premier. Harold Macmillan's evident incapacity during and after the Profumo scandal was in large measure responsible for the Conservative's subsequent defeat in 1964. As a party leader, in the narrower sense of the term, the Prime Minister must keep in close touch with his Parliamentary party, and, at elections and annual conferences, with the national organization of party activists. A Conservative premier can rely on a loyalty which his Labour counterpart must assiduously cultivate. The former also has less to fear from ideological snipers or potential rivals for the leadership.

As first Minister to the Crown, it is the Prime Minister who attends weekly meetings with the Monarch to keep her informed of Cabinet decisions and to receive the Monarch's spasmodic, but still significant, advice, encouragement, and warning. It is the Prime Minister, alone, who advises the Monarch on the date of Parliament's dissolution and, in the past, his opinion carried considerable weight over the appointment of his successor.

In the Commons, the premier sits on the Treasury Bench and, although he is expected to play a prominent role in debate, to attend more regularly than other Ministers, and to answer questions, his administrative responsibilities for ordering the business of the Commons are largely delegated to the Leader of the House and the Government Chief Whip. Finally, the premier acts as the chairman of the Commonwealth Conference whenever Britain plays host, and performs some ceremonial functions, though these are largely borne by the Monarch and Royal Family. Matters of 'high policy', like national security, are generally regarded as the personal prerogative of the Prime Minister and he has always taken the initiative on key issues such as the atomic bomb (Attlee), Suez (Eden), the EEC (Macmillan), and devaluation (Wilson). A Prime Minister may do more than his predecessors; the relentless evolution of the Constitution makes it hard for him to do less.

Consider the case for and against a smaller Cabinet.

The plea for a smaller Cabinet was first put forward by the Haldane Committee on the Machinery of Local Government which reported in 1918. Impressed by the efficiency of Lloyd George's War Cabinet, the Committee recommended that the institution be retained in peacetime and claimed that it would have a number of positive advantages: it would facilitate swift decision making; it would co-ordinate the activities of the various departments of state more efficiently; it would be better able to discern and impose financial priorities; and, freed from the clogging detail of day to day administration, it could concentrate its attention on the vital, and often neglected, task of long-range policy formulation. The recommendations of the Haldane Committee were subsequently reinforced by the arguments of L. S. Amery and the experience of 1916 to 1918 confirmed by that of 1940 to 1945. The increasing volume of government business strengthened the case put by the critics of the traditional Cabinet. Academic research supports the commonsense view that smaller bodies reach decisions faster than large ones. Many commentators have pointed out that the Cabinet in practice performs most of its functions *via* a vast complex of interlocking subcommittees, which, it is argued, strengthens the authority of the Prime Minister at the expense of the Cabinet as a whole.

The apparent strength of the case for a smaller Cabinet is weakened by the practical difficulties of bringing it into operation, as well as by the fact that the existing system has more virtues than its critics might care to admit. It is misleading, in the first instance, to argue the case for a smaller Cabinet on the basis of wartime experience, for in wartime party conflict, the essence of normal political life, is muted and decision making simplified by the overriding aim of victory. The small Cabinet would, inevitably, become a 'super Cabinet' and this would necessitate working out a new set of relationships between Ministers in the Cabinet and Ministers charged with the daily administration of the departments of state. On the one hand, there is the danger that every petty decision would be referred to the super Cabinet, overwhelming it with detail, and, on the other, the danger that departmental Ministers might seize the initiative to such an extent that the activities of the administration as a whole would become seriously dislocated, while the super Cabinet was relegated to a superfluous advisory role. Again, there is the problem of ministerial responsibility—who, in practice, would be accountable before the House for the activities of each particular government department? The claim that effective 'long-term' policy making can be effected without reference to the experience of daily administration, is dubious, as the impracticability of programmes, formulated by parties enjoying the enforced idleness of Opposition, bears witness.

Besides the problems which a small Cabinet would raise, there are positive advantages which would be lost if the present 'large' Cabinet were to be abolished. Neither party is monolithic or homogeneous; both are composed of factions based on personalities, ideology, interests, and policies. The Cabinet has its political, as well as its administrative aspect and a large Cabinet of 20 to 25 is better able to secure adequate representation for all the major party sub-groups than a small Cabinet of 5 to 6. In addition, the large Cabinet makes it possible to include relatively junior Ministers, enabling them to serve an 'apprenticeship' for the highest level of political activity.

A number of Prime Ministers have attempted to move in the direction of a smaller Cabinet, but the late Sir Winston Churchill's 'Overlord' experiment set the process back a decade while Harold Wilson found himself unable to make good his pre-election pledge to work through a Cabinet considerably smaller than that of Sir Alec Douglas-Home. The present Cabinet structure does have its defects, but in the tradition of our evolving Constitution, we are unlikely to see any drastic 'reform'. Instead, it is far more likely that even greater use will be made of Cabinet subcommittees, and even, as in the case of the long-term policy review 'think-tank' led by Lord Rothschild, of committees reporting to Cabinet subcommittees. The Cabinet secretariat will probably grow in size and efficiency and there will be more work for nondepartmental co-ordinating Ministers like the Lord President of the Council, the Chancellor of the Duchy of Lancaster and, indeed, the Prime Minister himself.

What is meant by 'collective responsibility'? Why is it important?

The convention of collective responsibility implies that all the members of a Government, and more particularly of a Cabinet, are collectively responsible for the success and failure of its policies and must support them before Parliament, party, and public. Ministers dissenting strongly from a particular policy must resign, as Frank Cousins did over the statutory regulation of wages, or as George Brown did, not over a particular policy, but rather over the way in which decisions were made, or as he alleged, not made by the Cabinet. Lord Melbourne summed it up when he said: 'It does not matter much what we say so long as we all say the same thing'.

The acknowledgement of the convention of collective responsibility enables a Government to present a united front to a hostile political world, eager to seize on divisions and dissensions. The united front is an essential prerequisite for the preservation of party discipline in the House and enables the Government to meet the onslaughts of the Opposition and the press without endangering its own stability by encouraging faction fights based on personal or ideological differences.

Junior Ministers are not exempt from this form of self-restraint and even unpaid Parliamentary Private Secretaries appear to be bound by it. In 1965, Mr F. Allaun resigned rather than publicly support government policy on Vietnam. In 1967, Harold Wilson obliged a number of PPSs to resign when they refused support for specific aspects of current economic policy. Only where 'moral' or 'social' issues are involved, where no 'party line' exists, are members of the Government allowed the luxury of a free vote and even in these situations an informal government consensus often exists.

The National Government's open decision to 'agree to differ' over tariffs is unique and can only be understood in the context of the exceptional circumstance of a coalition of Conservative, Liberal, and Labour members with fundamentally opposing views on a specific policy, but a collective determination to hold the coalition together in a time of national crisis. In fact, the 'agreement' lasted only from January to September 1932, when the free-traders, Snowden, Samuel, and Sinclair, resigned.

The existence of an acknowledged collective responsibility does not, however, necessarily mean that all members of the Government, or even of the Cabinet, are in unanimous agreement. In Opposition, every party feels free to reveal differences and divisions and this is not entirely due to post-electoral demoralization. In Government, men are held together by their need for mutual support in the face of the Opposition and many persuade themselves not to resign on any particular issue in the hope that by remaining in office they may possibly exercise some favourable influence on policy in the future.

Press and public do not take the unanimous pose at face value and some Ministers are certainly held to be more responsible than others. Munich (1938) and Suez (1956) were disasters which were ultimately placed at the door of particular Ministers. On the other hand, particular Ministers often identify themselves with a specific policy, as Sir Alec Douglas-Home did with sales of arms to South Africa. Some Ministers, like the Minister of Transport and the Chancellor of the Exchequer, can anticipate generally adverse public feeling most of the time, while Ministers pursuing a definite departmental policy, like comprehensive education, can expect particular attention from pressure groups. Identifying a particular Minister with a policy can also give the Cabinet some freedom to manoeuvre in difficult circumstances and translate collective into individual responsibility if it should become necessary to drop a particular line of policy—as in the case of the unfortunate Hoare in 1935. The forced resignation of Selwyn Lloyd after the failure of 'his' incomes policy in 1962 provides another example.

It is vital, however, to the continued life of a Government to maintain a general unity without which Parliamentary and electoral security will be gravely impaired. Patrick Gordon Walker has recently asserted (*The Cabinet* 1970) that an informally acknowledged convention—the 'leak'—enables Cabinet Ministers to adhere in public to a policy commitment, while indirectly assuring their followers inside and outside Parliament of their desire and intention to modify it if possible. Like so many other time-honoured conventions, collective responsibility is a constitutional fiction which serves the ends of party politics.

Discuss the development of administrative tribunals and the problems they have posed.

The courts of law, despite the wealth of experience they have accumulated in their long history, have proved inadequate to deal with many of the problems arising in a complex industrial society. Their leisurely procedures are really more fitted to the agrarian world in which they evolved. It has been necessary, therefore, over the last century, to create special tribunals to make quasi-judicial decisions over such matters as rents, workmen's compensation, or planning policies. As these tribunals have been created piecemeal to fulfil particular needs, their diverse origins are reflected in their diverse character and lack of common features. Some are permanent bodies like the Transport Tribunal or the Disciplinary Committee of the Law Society, and they have procedures similar to that of a court of law. Others, like the statutory tribunals created to settle disputes about National Insurance or state pensions, have more informal methods of working. Some, particularly where a specific planning decision is challenged, are appointed *ad hoc*. There are also 'tribunals' which are not tribunals at all in fact, but where a Minister or his department in effect makes the decisions in the normal course of business. Statutory tribunals have been growing rapidly and now exist for various aspects of agriculture, education, the National Health Service, and rate valuation, and numerous other matters subject to government regulation and control.

The growth of administrative tribunals and the extension of delegated legislation both owe their expansion to increased government activity in an age of collectivism. Tribunals exist to exercise discretionary powers in the light of fair-minded expertise and define such difficult concepts as 'a fair rent', 'adequate compensation', or 'a building of special achitectural interest', definitions which are better attempted by experts than judges, by people with experience of child welfare work or civil engineering rather than of the law as such. The basic justifications for the existence of administrative tribunals are necessity (the courts would have been overwhelmed by the half million applications for postponement of National Service alone), cheapness (no fees or expensive counsel), and speed (no lengthy documentation or elaborate calling of witnesses).

On the other hand, it must be remembered that these tribunals differ from the courts of law in a number of important ways: Ministers may in practice act as judges of their own case; parties involved may not always have the chance of a hearing; the person making the decision may not even be identifiable and the grounds for the decision left unstated. Perhaps the most alarming aspects of the system are that so few people are aware of their existence and that their activities receive so little publicity, though press coverage of the Immigration Appeals Tribunal's handling of the Dutschke case may have gone some way towards changing this. Above all, it is a matter for concern, not pride as A. V. Dicey believed, that we have no body of administrative law like France to protect the individual in his dealings with the state.

The situation was, however, improved by the Franks Committee investigation. Their report, published in 1959, criticized the combination of executive and adjudicatory functions and insisted on the need for settled rules of procedure. It proposed two advisory councils, one for England and Wales and the other for Scotland, to exercise a general oversight of tribunals and recommended publication of inspectors' reports, the right of all to be legally represented before tribunals, and the possibility of appeal to an appelate tribunal and, on a point of law, to the courts. Government endorsement of this report undoubtedly raised standards of openness and impartiality. More settled procedures have been evolved, but the Crowther Commission could well add a review of the need for an administrative body to its long list of constitutional problems for further consideration.

Local government

What were the main findings and recommendations of the *report on the management of local government*?

The tone of the report was generally critical, as evidenced by the title of the opening section, *'The Urgent Need for Reform'*. The report stated that there are, in Britain, some 40 000 local councillors, sitting on 1450 councils, employing just under 2 million people, and spending £3000 million a year, yet the nation, it alleged, was not receiving full value for money in either financial or human terms.

In its analysis of the causes of this situation, the report dealt only briefly with the complex and illogical structure of local government which carved up 'regions' and obscured functions and responsibilities, as the Commission chaired by Lord Redcliffe-Maud was already examining this aspect of the problem in detail. The root of the problem, the report stated, lay in the perpetuation of the nineteenth-century tradition that councillors should concern themselves with day to day administrative decisions. This made it necessary to establish large numbers of time consuming committees, which kept councillors from their constituents and were not efficient in reaching decisions. Work became fragmented between a large number of poorly co-ordinated departments; councillors become obsessed with detail at the expense of general strategy; permanent officials felt stifled and unable to use their initiative or exploit their expertise to the benefit of the community. The faulty functioning of the local government machine meant that local authorities were distrusted by Parliament and Whitehall, which tended to control their actions ever more closely and reduce them to the role of subordinate agents. This discouraged potentially invaluable persons from serving either as councillors or as officials. As a result of all these factors, the gulf between governors and governed at the local level continued to widen.

Regarding the internal organization of local councils, the report recommended that there should be a clear division of work between councillors and permanent officials; that councillors should restrict their attention to major policies and delegate powers of routine decision making; that committees should not number more than 6, should have no more than 15 members, and should limit themselves to discussion, not administration; and that the whole structure should be controlled by a management board of 5 to 9 members, with wide powers, which would act as the sole link between the council and its committees, would formulate proposals for council approval, and would exercise overall powers of supervision. Members of the management board should be paid up to £1000 a year, and its chief officer should be a clerk, with managerial rather than legal training.

In dealing with relations between central and local government, the report was equally radical, emphasizing the need to reverse the trend toward using local authorities as the agents of Whitehall. It recommended that local authorities should be free to determine their own internal structure, freed of statutory requirements to establish certain committees; that they should be free to appoint and dismiss their principal officers without Ministry approval; that details of expenditure should be left to local authority discretion; that their taxing powers should be increased; and that they should be given powers of 'general competence' rather than having to depend on Parliament for grants of specific powers. A local government central office should also be set up to represent the common interest of local authorities to government and the public and to provide research and information services for councillors, officers, and the press.

Finally, the report dealt with ways of promoting closer relations between local authorities and the public they serve. The main recommendations were that elections for *all* local authorities should be held triennially on the same day throughout the country, which would attract more publicity, and promote a higher turnout and more contests; that councils should not have more than 75 members and that aldermen should be abolished; that no person over 70 should be allowed to stand at elections; that up to one-third of committee members should be co-opted; that councillors should make greater efforts to reach the public; and that an educational programme should be conducted *via* schools and should include training courses for both teachers and local councillors. Above all, the report stressed that the co-operation of the news media was vital since closing the gulf depended upon projecting a favourable 'image' to the public. Councils should, therefore, regard journalists as allies rather than potential enemies. Press rooms and free telephones should be made available for them and 'White' and 'Green' Papers should be circulated in advance of major decisions in order to stimulate public discussion. The value of the report lies in the fact that its recommendations can be largely implemented without major changes in the structure of local government. The main failing of the report is that its implementation rests on the enthusiasm and efficiency it seeks to create.

Consider the reasons for and against becoming a local councillor.

Giving up his own time is the greatest sacrifice the councillor is called upon to make. According to the survey conducted for the Committee on the Management of Local Government, the average councillor spends 52 hours per month on council business. County councillors may spend as much as 76 hours per month. Closer analysis reveals that for the energetic and conscientious councillor, that is about 2 out of every 3, the burden is even greater as he is likely to attend more committee meetings and take more care over his 'paperwork' than some of his more passive colleagues. The indications are that this burden is likely to grow rather than diminish as the councillor's length of service increases, as time saved through acquired expertise will be more than offset by time involved in increased responsibilities, like the chairmanship of key committees. Social and family life are almost bound to suffer in consequence.

There are also considerable financial disadvantages to be considered. A councillor *can* claim for travelling, subsistence, and loss of earnings, but minor items like telephone calls, stationery, and charitable donations all add up and are not, in practice, claimed. For the self-employed councillor, loss of time, attending to council business, may well mean loss of income; for the employed man, assiduous attendance at council meetings could mean being passed over for promotion. At least one GLC councillor, elected in 1970, was instantly dismissed by his employer.

Involvement in 'party politics' may dissuade some. But about half of all councillors are returned unopposed, without the formality of a ballot. This occurs mostly in rural areas. This should enable some potential councillors to overcome the obstacle of party politics. Others could serve as co-opted members of committees. More use could certainly be made of the aldermanic system to recruit 'independents', rather than to save party 'faithfuls' from the rigours of electioneering.

Finally, on the debit side it might be claimed by some that service on a local council is simply not worth the bother as all power rests in Whitehall and Westminster and the councillor can seldom really *do* anything. The recent spate of Royal Commissions, reports, and academic publications on the role and organization of local government suggests, on the contrary, that local government is very much alive and there are powerful interests concerned to make it more effective in action and more satisfying to those who serve their community.

Council service does have its positive aspects. Most councillors derive great satisfaction from helping people to solve their problems, particularly housing and welfare problems. In addition, council work enables many people to utilize talents which cannot find a useful outlet elsewhere and would otherwise lie dormant. Both these benefits were emphasized in H. H. Heclo's survey of 29 councillors on Manchester City Council (*Journal of Public Administration*, Summer 1969), though he did also point out that many councillors were frustrated in their role as policy makers, not because opportunities were lacking, but because their lack of expertise prevented them from making full use of these opportunities and obliged them to rely heavily on the permanent officials. It may be that the introduction of salaries for councillors will remove a disincentive which currently discourages younger managers, executives, and professional men from putting their expert knowledge and ability at the service of the community and will thus lead to the recruitment of more councillors confident of their capacity to contribute to policy making in such areas as planning, education, and environmental control.

How can local government benefit from modern methods of management?

Local authorities enjoy a monopoly position and, having no competitors, can never go bankrupt. It is true that they remain under the watchful eyes of the Ministry in Whitehall and, closer at hand, the district auditor, but there are no adequate criteria by which to judge whether services are being provided as efficiently as possible or whether the ratepayer is getting value for money. Local authorities do not have entirely comparable problems to those of industry and so analogies must be drawn with care. They are charged with providing a wide range of services and performing numerous statutory duties; their revenue is relatively inelastic; they are answerable to both the central government and the local electors; their actions are bound by statute and their recruitment policies hampered by inflexible salary scales and required qualifications. Their most pressing problem, as J. P. Mackintosh emphasizes in the first chapter of *The Devolution of Power*, is a critical shortage of executive staff with appropriate managerial skills and experience. His remedy is the creation of regional units to give officials more scope for initiative and larger salaries. The Committee on the Management of Local Government suggested a number of less fundamental steps that could be taken to improve the efficiency of local government, notably the creation of work study departments and the recruitment of town clerks with managerial rather than legal qualifications.

Where management consultants have been employed, results have been startling. The old metropolitan borough of Wandsworth paid a £9999 fee, in return for which savings of £20 000 were effected in one year, £30 000 the next year, and £40 000 in the third, and every subsequent year. The experience of Mansfield, Notts, was similarly encouraging—a saving of some £20 000 on the annual rates bill and the provision of extra services valued at £40 000. The re-structuring of dustmen's rounds led to an improvement in the service and a 30 per cent reduction in the labour force, making possible higher individual wages supplemented by efficiency payments and a lower overall wage bill.

One firm, S. J. Noel Brown & Co., specializes in consultation services for local government and gave evidence before the Maud Commission. Consultants survey existing procedures and then make and help to implement recommendations designed to cut down paperwork, eliminate duplication of effort, save man hours, and establish clear criteria for operational efficiency. On the whole, their operations have raised morale as well as efficiency and have made officials keen to operate their own permanent 'O and M' and work study section. Consultants also offer appointments services, giving local authorities the opportunity to recruit from industry and use the skills of experienced personnel selection experts, rather than trust to the local press and a specially convened committee of reluctant councillors.

The appointment of Frank Harris, a former executive of the Ford Motor Company, as 'city manager' of Newcastle-upon-Tyne, in 1965, marked a milestone in local government history. Freed from departmental responsibilities and ceremonial functions, Mr Harris was able to concentrate on co-ordinating the general strategy of community development. Although he resigned in 1969, his relatively brief 'reign' may mark the beginning of the end of the solicitors' traditional monopoly of the position of chief executive officer. The fact that Leicester, Basildon, and West Sussex have now advertised for clerks without legal qualifications shows that Newcastle's lead is being followed. The London boroughs now have their own Management Services Committee; Coventry runs its own internal O and M unit. Berkshire, Oxfordshire, and Reading have set up a joint management services unit and it is hoped that other small authorities will follow their example and pool resources to appoint experts or share a computer. Management consultants naturally have an interest in spreading information about the contribution modern techniques can make in such diverse fields as planning, housing, measuring traffic flow, buying supplies, recruiting personnel, and general financial control. The Institute of Local Government Studies in Birmingham, the Local Government Research Unit, the Local Government Information Office, and the Local Government Chronicle are all helping to diffuse knowledge of modern management applications to the field of local government. The appointment of well qualified public relations and press officers could help to reinforce this healthy trend by enlisting the support of local ratepayers who will benefit from cheaper and more efficient services and, it is to be hoped, increased rather than diminished democratic control.

How could local government finance be reformed?

The revenue sources of local government, like so many of its arrangements, are largely the product of chance and circumstance rather than of reason and policy. In consequence, local authorities often find themselves turning more and more to central government for funds and this naturally implies a diminution in their power to act on their own initiative. Rates, formerly the main source of income, now provide less than half of what local authorities need and the rating system itself is frequently criticized as inequitable and inefficient. Unlike personal taxation, it takes no account of variations in income or family responsibilities and is, therefore, very often regressive in operation, discriminating against the poor, and particularly those with large families. Rates are also an inelastic source of revenue as valuation is a complex, expensive process undertaken rather infrequently. Local government responsibilities increase every year and electors expect services to be uniformly administered throughout the country, whether their particular local authority is rich or poor. Unless radical steps are taken to reform local government finance, it will continue to atrophy until local authorities are completely dependent on Whitehall and Westminster.

Many reforms have been suggested: few have been tried. Discussion has tended to focus on the difficulties rather than the potentialities of reform. The Liberal Party, for instance, favours rating not of buildings, but of site values. A study group of the Royal Institute of Public Administration has suggested that local authorities should be empowered to levy a local income tax which could be collected *via* local employers. The objections to this are obvious—taxation in respect of workplaces rather than homes, and discrimination in favour of towns at the expense of commuter and suburban areas. These are not, however, insurmountable problems. Successive Royal Commissions have commented on the desirability of widening the tax base. Concrete suggestions and a definite lead have been lacking.

Rating of empty property could be introduced. The City of London Corporation obtained power to levy rates on empty property by Act of Parliament and it would be possible to extend the principle to sites awaiting development and empty office blocks. This would scarcely be a radical reform and might simply put off the evil day by enabling the present system to limp on a little longer. The same might be said of proposals to re-impose rates on agricultural land and buildings.

Some of the heaviest burdens on local authorities, notably education, the police force, and roads, are subsidized by central government grants. It might reasonably be argued that these services are more national than local in character and their whole cost should, therefore, be borne by the Exchequer. The problem here would be to ensure that local control over such important matters was not totally compromised. One suggestion that has been made is to re-allocate existing sources of revenue, e.g., by transferring the revenue from motor vehicle licences to local authorities. Alternative suggestions include new local taxes on entertainment, bicycles, and restaurant meals. The experience of other European countries might provide us with possible answers to our current problem, but a solution must come soon.

'Party politics should have no place in local government.'   Discuss.

The arguments against party involvement in local politics are strong. Where elections are held on a local basis, only party sponsored candidates have any real hope of success and where one party is dominant in a particular ward or district, which is often the case, selection by the local party committee is tantamount to election. Electors, accustomed to voting on party lines, tend to know and care little about the personal qualities of candidates, and sometimes, as in 1967, use the local election simply as an opportunity to register a protest vote against the Government of the day, without thought or reference to local circumstances. The national parties have encouraged this as a means of demonstrating popular opinion and achieving control of local authorities as a countervailing power with which to block the implementation of central government policies, e.g., on comprehensive education. The dominance of party may, moreover, discourage potential, nonpartisan councillors from coming forward and this limits the field of recruitment. Parties in power are accused of taking 'real' decisions in a private caucus, thus reducing formal meetings to a facade.

There are, however, plenty of arguments on the other side. Party activity does increase interest in local elections; where parties are most vigorous turnout tends to be high. Party conflict also tends to reduce the number of unopposed elections (still reckoned at nearly 45 per cent by the Committee on the Management of Local Government). Furthermore, if a candidate is returned unopposed without a party label, it does not follow that he has no party loyalties, merely that he has not declared them. Politics, and indeed democracy, are about disagreements and conflicts of interest and, in most systems, these are crystallized into broad party allegiances. In a sense, therefore, to abolish party would be to abolish politics. Since local government does involve real decisions about education, housing, and planning, and ultimately about people and their welfare, it cannot be treated simply as an administrative function. Parties, rather than councillors, represent public opinion to which they are responsible. Where the business of a local authority is conducted on a party basis, its policies are more likely to be planned and consistent than policies dependent upon the unorganized and changing views of individual councillors.

The involvement of party is not, however, an 'either/or' question, but rather one of degree. In some councils, particularly rural ones, party loyalty has little significance beyond the actual election period —largely because the councillors are all of one mind and can act as independents because there is a strong consensus on fundamentals. There are no group meetings and aldermen and committee chairmen are chosen without much reference to formal allegiances. At the other extreme, in urban, industrial areas, party governs all, e.g., voting on committees, and the nomination of the chairmen and aldermen. Discipline is enforced by threats of expulsion, which, in effect, will mean loss of the seat at the next election. This situation is most common in county boroughs, particularly where Labour influence is strong. Intermediate situations naturally exist, where, for instance, party loyalties are strong but no group has an overall majority of seats. Where party is strong, however, it does serve to limit the power of local officials who are excluded from the 'caucus' meetings and would be obliged to take much more responsibility on their own shoulders in the absence of coherent party policies, evolved by group discussion and supported by firm majorities. Equally, the presence of the permanent officials, and the control exerted by Westminster and Whitehall prevent changes of electoral fortune from being translated into too violent disruptions of policy.

The law

Consider the cases for and against the present jury system.

The jury is one of the most ancient of British institutions and venerated as the bulwark of our most fundamental liberties. Once judges were regarded with suspicion, as instruments of the Crown, and the jury was correspondingly valued as free from political pressure. The trial of the Seven Bishops and the behaviour of the infamous Judge Jeffries in the reign of James II both seem to give clear evidence of this. The Bill of Rights, the Act of Settlement, and nearly three centuries of accumulated convention stand between ourselves and that time. The jury may seem less fundamental now that the independence of the judiciary is so firmly assured.

Many criticisms may be made of the jury system. Juries, being susceptible to emotion, are more likely to be swayed by the rhetoric of skilled counsel, than the trained and impartial mind of a judge. Since jurors rarely come into contact with crime, they are likely to lose sight of their main task, assessing the probability of guilt, and become blinded by their horror at the nature of the alleged crime itself. A trained legal mind, familiar enough with crime to have become objective in its approach, might be supposed to give accused persons more rational and consistent treatment. In civil cases, juries often find themselves lost in the tangled complexities of the law, finance, and commercial morality and custom. In the awarding of damages, juries are notoriously inconsistent. Finally, the property qualification for jury service ensures that, in practice, most jurors are male, middle aged, middle class, and socially conservative.

The arguments for the retention of the jury system, in some form, are, however, very strong, particularly if its role in civil cases is limited. It is reasonable that the prosecution must establish proof of its case in a manner comprehensible to the ordinary citizen. This strengthens the faith of every citizen in the legal system and this is, in itself, the strongest foundation of the rule of law. It is a tribute to our legal system that at a time when the popular reputation of politicians is as low as it ever has been, and many informed commentators speak of 'the decline of Parliament', the prestige of British justice is as high as it ever has been. In cases like slander and defamation, where the reality of the crime depends on the interpretations of words or actions by the man in the street, a jury is not simply useful but essential. In criminal cases juries err on the side of the accused and this ensures that, despite the practical disadvantages ensuing from it, the liberty and rights of the accused citizen are upheld. As government becomes increasingly bureaucratic and remote, it is important that no opportunities for citizen participation are prematurely curtailed by a shortsighted desire for administrative efficiency at the expense of public confidence.

In what ways have the courts acted to uphold the rule of law?

The basis of the rule of law, as A. V. Dicey formulated it, is the implication that legal rules are certain and thus that the rights of individuals and the behaviour of public authorities shall not be subject to arbitrary alteration. No punishment may, therefore, be imposed unless a breach of law has been established in a court of law. The rule of law also implies that everyone is subject to the law and may not plead deference to the orders of a superior as a defence for illegal acts, or claim to be tried by a special court under a separate code dealing with administrative actions. Civil servants and policemen can be arraigned before the ordinary law of the land for acts committed by them in their official capacities, just as though they were the acts of an ordinary citizen.

Our basic personal liberties are, to a large extent, the result of judicial decisions over a number of centuries, based on the incorruptibility of judges, their resistance to executive encroachment, and the orderly development of the law itself. The courts have continually refused to acknowledge *raison d'etat* as a substitute for legality and have upheld the right of a citizen to bring an action for damages for false imprisonment. The jury system has acted as a bulwark against arbitrary behaviour, but more fundamental, perhaps, has been the writ of *Habeas Corpus*, an order to 'produce the body' of any person suspected of being unlawfully detained. The writ of *Habeas Corpus* extends not only to British citizens but to all on British soil, with the exception of persons enjoying diplomatic immunity or coming under the terms of the visiting Forces Act, 1952, e.g., American servicemen. The writ may be suspended by emergency legislation, but this is very rare.

The three prerogative writs of Certiorari, Prohibition, and Mandamus have also been invaluable in safeguarding personal rights. The order of Certiorari commands judges and officers of inferior courts to bring a suit to the High Court either to ensure a fairer trial or to see whether the lower court has jurisdiction or to quash an order made by a court without jurisdiction. The order of Prohibition stops an inferior court from hearing a suit when it is outside its jurisdiction. The order of Mandamus directs an inferior court, or a person, or a corporation to do its duty, whether it be to compel authorities to perform certain undertakings or produce their accounts or to compel a lawful election where irregularities have occurred. Resistance to these orders is punishable as a form of contempt. Finally, the fact that the interpretation of the Common Law, with its assumption that all actions are legal unless specifically prohibited, lies in the hands of an impartial and respected authority is itself the greatest guarantee that the rights of the citizen and the law which upholds them will be universally respected.

How does the British Constitution protect the personal liberty of the individual?

The British Constitution recognizes no 'right' in the strict sense and construes liberty as the freedom an individual retains subject to the limitations of Common Law, Acts of Parliament, and local bylaws. At first sight, this appears to place individual personal liberty at the mercy of Parliament; in practice, the influence of public opinion, the vigilance of the Opposition, and the restrictive attitude of the courts towards legislation curtailing personal liberty, all help to maintain this most basic of the citizen's rights.

Every imprisonment or arrest is *prima facie* unlawful and must be justified before an appointed court on the grounds of: arrest and detention pending trial on a specific charge of crime; or, conviction and sentence for a specific offence after trial by a court of competent jurisdiction; or, custody pending extradition or deportation; or, committal for Contempt of Court or Parliament. Remedies for wrongful deprivation of liberty include: application for a writ of *habeas corpus;* appeal to a higher court against conviction and sentence; a civil action for damages for assault, false imprisonment, or malicious prosecution; a criminal prosecution for assault. The Common Law recognizes the right of the individual to use a reasonable amount of force in defence of himself and his household and this extends to resisting unlawful arrest without a warrant. In practice, it would be wiser to pursue a remedy after arrest by a police officer rather than resist an arrest, which might, upon examination, turn out to be technically lawful.

The most efficient remedy is the writ of *habeas corpus*, requested from the High Court by the detained person or his legal adviser. If the High Court, upon investigation, decides that the detention is unlawful, it will order the prisoner's immediate release. Applications for such a writ may be made in case of necessity (at night, at weekends, or during law vacation) to a judge in Chambers. *Habeas Corpus* can only be suspended by Act of Parliament, which is done very rarely indeed.

The powers of the police regarding the liberty of the individual are limited by the 1964 Police Act which provides that a Chief Constable is liable to be sued for torts committed by officers under his control. (Damages and costs are payable out of the local police fund.) Unless arrested and charged with a specific crime, the citizen has no obligation to identify himself to the police, answer questions, or accompany them to a police station; in practice, law-abiding citizens co-operate fully with the police. Police officers may make arrests without a warrant for breaches of the peace committed in their presence, for wilful obstruction of the highway, and where the officer reasonably suspects a person of committing an 'arrestable' offence. Police questioning procedure is regulated by the Judge's Rules, which are not rules of law, but their non-observance would lead the court to reject, as inadmissible evidence, statements made by the accused. The purpose of Judge's Rules is to prevent, by requiring frequent 'cautions', extortion of information or confessions by threats or offers of reward. Witnesses are similarly free to answer police questions, although they may be compelled by a *subpoena* to give evidence in proceedings before a court.

Preventive detention is also illegal, as is extended detention before trial. Magistrates have discretionary authority over the granting of bail to persons accused of serious offences. There is a right of appeal to the High Court if a person committed for trial at a superior court is refused bail. The National Council for Civil Liberties alleges that JPs sometimes pre-judge accused persons, particularly students and demonstrators, and refuse bail to 'give them a taste of prison'. Vigilance on the part of the press and the High Court is necessary if such abuses are to remain exceptions to the wise and humane practice of the Common Law.

What limitations are there on freedom of speech in Britain?

Freedom of speech is the right to express opinions, orally or in writing, provided that the law is not infringed. Associated with it are rights of freedom of conscience and worship. The most significant aspects of this freedom are: the liberty to express and propagate political views, including criticism of the Government; freedom of debate in Parliament; the immunity of judges, counsel, jury, and witnesses taking part in judicial proceedings; and the privilege of publishing fair and accurate reports of Parliamentary debates and trials. The law is infringed by such offences as treason, seditious libel, provoking public disorder, breaches of the official Secrets Acts, incitement of the armed forces or police to mutiny, Contempt of Court, by the tort of libel or slander, and by Contempt of Parliament. No censorship exists in English law in the sense that the written word must receive the prior approval of an official body before publication. Censorship of stage plays disappeared in 1968.

Prosecution for seditious libel was a valuable political weapon in the early nineteenth century, but is rare nowadays and in practice only instituted when there is incitement to violence. It is not seditious to suggest that the Government has been mistaken, that the Constitution is imperfect, or that the laws should be changed. Successful prosecution also depends upon proof of intention to promote violence, not simple cause and effect.

The strict law of libel is a strong defence of the individual and his reputation and a necessary counterweight to the power of the press, which has a vested interest in publishing whatever will make a good 'story'. Newspapers do enjoy a few minor legal concessions in recognition of the fact that they have to be produced at high speed, but there is no special freedom of the press, nor any right for journalists to obtain information by methods forbidden to a private citizen, e.g., trespass and nuisance. Nor may journalists refuse to divulge sources of information when called as witnesses. In practice, courts pass over this aspect unless it is considered relevant and essential. The imprisonment of three journalists after the Vassall Tribunal of Inquiry in 1963 shows that courts will not content themselves with threats in cases of defiance.

The Official Secrets Act, 1911, has been much criticized for limiting freedom to gather and publish information. 'National security' and 'public interest' have become rather blurred. As it stands, the law provides an impenetrable cloak which disguises much that is merely embarrassing to governments and state departments rather than material to national security. Similarly, the law relating to Contempt of Court must not be so pettishly interpreted as to limit genuine criticism of judicial conduct, made in good faith and not imputing improper motives.

'British justice may be impartially administered but only the rich can afford it.'   Comment.

It is more than forty years since Lord Justice Darling remarked that the Law Courts, like the Ritz Hotel, are open to all, and his observation has lost none of its ironic implications. There is still an urgent need to make litigation cheaper and quicker and make it possible for every person to defend his or her rights, regardless of personal circumstances. A great deal could be done to reduce the cost of going to law, particularly the abolition of the distinction between solicitors and barristers, which obliges litigants to employ two skilled advisers whose long and expensive training must be paid for by those who employ their services. It should also be possible to decentralize some of the work of the higher courts and reduce the number of occasions on which proceedings must be held in London, involving the expense and delay of bringing witnesses to court. Greater efforts could also be made to settle out of court and perhaps a small claims court could be set up to deal with cases involving sums of money under £25, where legal fees would normally exceed the amount involved. This would be of great benefit to persons on low incomes, particularly widows and pensioners who can ill afford to lose even a small sum.

The legal aid system leaves a great deal to be desired. At present, it is administered under the terms of the Poor Prisoner's Defence Act, 1930, the Summary Jurisdiction (Appeals) Act, 1933, and the Legal Aid and Advice Act, 1949. Aside from the fact that a candidate for aid must satisfy a National Assistance Committee that his income and capital fall below certain low statutory limits, he must also satisfy a local Law Society Committee that his case is reasonable. Such evidence as exists suggests that interpretations of what is 'reasonable' vary from area to area and there is certainly a strong case for revising the income limits to take account of postwar inflation. At present, it has been said that only the very rich and the destitute can afford to go to law and most citizens fall into neither category. Theoretical rights are no rights at all and justice which cannot be obtained in practice cannot be said to exist in practice. There are, of course, other expedients. The National Council for Civil Liberties disburses some funds to fight cases involving basic principles of individual rights. Sometimes a newspaper will take up a case, though usually for the 'news value' rather than to support any important principle involved. Trade unions and professional associations will often pay legal costs where their members' rights are concerned, and a number of specialized interest groups, like the AA, maintain legal departments which will give free advice to members. Release takes up the cause of drug addicts, Shelter goes to court on behalf of squatters and the homeless, but pensioners, widows, and consumers are still weakly represented in this way. An increasing number of young lawyers are following the transatlantic example and giving a really professional 'Citizen's Advice Bureau' service for the poor, immigrants, and other underprivileged minorities. The rapid growth of these organizations in the last decade or so shows both a general desire to see justice done and the inadequacy of the present legal system to secure it for all members of our society.

How are JPs recruited and trained? Could the system be improved?

New appointments to the bench are ultimately the responsibility of the Lord Chancellor's office, but any organization or individual may make a nomination to the local advisory committee *via* its secretary, the only member whose name is made public. Nominations from local branches of political parties are usual and this makes the construction of politically balanced benches easier. Recommendations are passed from the advisory committee to the Lord Chancellor, who makes the final decision after his staff has conducted a discreet investigation into the background and character of the candidate. There is no formal investigation of the attitudes of applicants, however. Unsuccessful applications are rejected without explanation, successful candidates are appointed permanently.

Training consists of three attendances at court for a total of not less than six hours in all and a course of six elementary lectures. After this, the JP may begin to sit on the bench, though he will obviously be very much in the hands of his more experienced colleagues and his real training will, in effect, have entered a stage of practical 'apprenticeship'. The second formal stage of training consists of visits to two penal institutions and six more detailed lectures to fill in the magistrate's knowledge of court procedure, rules of evidence, and sentencing. Training was not made compulsory until 1966, despite the recommendation of the 1948 Royal Commission.

Critics of the present recruiting procedure focus their attention on the fact that the process is secret and most of the appointees are elderly, retired persons, largely from the middle and upper classes. Instead they suggest election and the introduction of realistic expenses to enable younger persons and working men and women to be considered for office. This would, they claim, make the members of the bench more in touch with the world on which they pass judgement. Appointment for a limited period of, say, five years, would make it possible to review performance on the bench and provide the opportunity to refuse renewal of tenure if necessary. Bringing down the compulsory retirement age would oblige advisory committees to search more widely for potential recruits. Training could be improved by extending the number of observer sessions to a dozen, by instituting formal examinations, and perhaps by including 'mock' trials. The 'syllabus' could be enlivened and improved by including discussions with those involved in the prevention and treatment of crime at all levels: the police force, social workers, teachers, barristers, etc. The results would be less reliance on the Clerk of the Court and greater consistency in sentencing. The same end could be more simply, but more expensively, obtained by increasing the number of stipendiaries.

The Talbot Press (S.P.C.K.), Saffron Walden, Essex   13236